trojan women

a collection of essays edited by
david stuttard and tamsin shasha

aod publications • york

published by
aod publications

© **aod** 2001

actors of dionysus,
26 charlton street, york, uk yo23 1jn

t +44 1904 642 912
f +44 1904 541 749
e info@actorsofdionysus.com
www.actorsofdionysus.com

Contents

Acknowledgements

aod thanks Cambridge University Press for permission to reprint the extract (slightly adapted) from Chapter 7 of the Cambridge Companion to Greek Tragedy, ed. P.E.Easterling, Cambridge 1997 (173-7).

References

In her article, Womens' Voices, Womens' Hands, Ruth Hazel refers to the following works:

Barlow, S. A., *Euripides: Trojan Women*
        Warminster, 1986
Casson, J., *Lewis and Sybil: A Memoir*
        London, 1972
Kennelly, B., *The Trojan Women*
        Newcastle-upon-Tyne, 1993

Foreword

David Stuttard & Tamsin Shasha

Trojan Women was first performed at the Great Festival of Dionysus in Athens in 415 BC. The only surviving play from a trilogy whose action spanned the whole of the Trojan War, its subject is the fate of the women captured when Troy was sacked by the Greeks.

Euripides focuses on four women in particular: the old Hekabe, former queen of Troy; her virgin daughter, Cassandra; her daughter-in-law (the mother of her grandson), Andromache; and the sultry Helen whose infidelity with Hekabe's son, Paris, sparked off the conflict in the first place.

While Hekabe remains a constant presence, the other women are paraded in front of the audience like lots in a slave auction - or the three contestants in that infamous beauty contest, the Judgement of Paris, in which lay the origins of the war.

As in that contest, the same female archetypes are present: the virgin (Athene/Cassandra), the mother (Hera/Andromache) and the whore (Aphrodite/Helen). As in that contest, too, it is the whore who wins out in the end.

The bulk of the action is played out on a human level, with the fate of the women being decided by their victorious Greek masters. But casting a shadow over the entire play is the decision of the gods, Athene and Poseidon, (known by the audience but not by the characters on stage) to destroy the Greek fleet on its voyage home. In the midst of victory, disaster looms.

From even this summary it is apparent that *Trojan Women* raises important questions concerning not only human relationships and gender issues, but also the morality of war and how far mankind can control events before they spiral out of all control. They are questions which are as central to the way we live our lives today as they were to Euripides' audience two and a half millennia ago.

It was in an attempt to address many of these questions, alongside more general questions of Greek tragedy, that we asked some of the leading classicists in the British Isles today to contribute to this collection of essays.

Our thanks to them all for their excellent and enthusiastic response, to the Classical Association and the Jowett Copyright Trustees for helping to fund this project and to all at Hamilton Printing, Hull for their invaluable help and advice.

York, September 2001

trojan women

Who Was to Blame?

Sir Kenneth Dover

Troy has at last fallen. All its grown men have been killed in (or after) the fighting, King Priam among them. Now all its women and children become slaves, chattels, at the absolute disposal of their Greek conquerors. Hecuba, the widowed Queen of Troy, now discovers what it is like to be a slave. So does Andromache, widow of Hecuba's son Hector, the man who had been Troy's most valiant defender; so too Cassandra, whom Homer calls "the most beautiful of the daughters of Priam", now allocated as a concubine to the Greek commander Agamemnon.

Trojan Women does not offer us a sequence of events which can be called a "plot" in the usual sense of that word; no suspense, no surprises, no impasse or conflict requiring resolution by a *deus ex machina*, no "creative" mythology. We are presented only with the familiar, predictable sequence which belongs to the capture of a city, or rather, to its immediate aftermath, from the herding of the captives to the conflagration of the emptied city with which the play ends. But within this relentless accumulation of brutalities and sorrows we strike a hard core of argument: *whose fault* was the Trojan War? The question is one which attracted the attention not only of poets, from Homer onwards, but also of a historian (Herodotus) and a sophist (Gorgias) in Euripides' own time and an orator (Isocrates) soon after.

The essentials of the myth were exceedingly familiar to Euripides' Athenian audience from poetry and the visual arts, however varied the details of its treatment by individuals. The goddesses Hera, Athena and Aphrodite demanded of Paris, a son of Priam, that he judge which of them was the most beautiful (a trio of deities, witches - as in *Macbeth* - or goblins, with a set of three prophecies, gifts, promises or threats, is a common structure in the mythology of many cultures). Paris gave the prize to Aphrodite, and his reward from her was the most beautiful woman in the world, Helen, wife of Menelaus, king of Sparta. Paris's opportunity came when he stayed as a guest at Sparta in Menelaus's absence; he and Helen went back to Troy together, and there they stayed, Priam refusing to surrender Helen, until a combination of Greek cities and tribes conquered Troy at the end of a ten-year war.

In *Trojan Women* Helen is naturally among the captives, and Menelaus orders her to be brought out that he may confront her in Hecuba's presence. His opening words declare that his purpose in fighting the war was not simply to regain his wife but to inflict on Troy just punishment for condoning Paris's violation, gravely offensive to Zeus, of the laws of hospitality. This declaration not only establishes Menelaus's claim to piety and righteousness but also pre-empts a defence against the accusation (on which more below) "What, all *that* just to recover Helen?" Certainly the offence was there; yet in the *Odyssey*, Helen, so far from being punished by her injured husband, lives with him happily ever after. Modern readers of the *Iliad* may be forgiven for feeling that it treats the abduction of a beautiful wife on rather the same level as the theft of a prestigious possession - say, a racehorse; we don't punish the horse for being stolen, we just try to get it back. (The implied attitude is not peculiar to archaic Greece; only a few years ago a very successful businessman boasted to a newspaper that he now had "a Rolls, a beautiful wife, and a yacht").

According to popular Greek belief Menelaus, apprehending Helen when Troy fell, discarded his sword and his vengeful intent when she bared her incomparable breasts. In *Trojan Women* Euripides solves - or, if you will, evades - the problem of reconciling immovably established legend with the prevailing moral sentiment of his time; his Menelaus takes Helen back to Sparta with the avowed intention of executing her there (an oddly unconvincing refinement). It is left to the audience, prompted by Hecuba's warning of the deadly power of female beauty over men, to recall what "really" (i.e. in the *Odyssey*) happened.

Menelaus's threat elicits from Helen a demand to be allowed to speak in her own defence, a demand to which he yields at

3

Hecuba's request, and it is in fact Hecuba, not Menelaus, who takes on the role of Helen's adversary in the rhetorical showpiece which follows. Helen does not deny that she fell in love with Paris, but it must be confessed that her apologia is poor stuff, a display of unconvincing sophistries easily and scornfully rebutted by Hecuba. At one point Helen even employs a vulgar argument which a few years earlier Aristophanes had caricatured by putting it in the mouth of Wrong, the personification of sophistic immorality: "If you're caught in bed with someone else's wife... you can point to Zeus and say that sexual love is too much for *him* - and how can you, a mortal, be stronger than a god?"

Unlike Hecuba in Euripides, Priam in the *Iliad* is strikingly courteous and compassionate in his dealings with Helen. "I don't hold you to blame", he tells her, "it is the *gods* that I blame". It would be a mistake to treat his words as a logically defensible outcome of hard theological thinking, let alone as expressing the settled opinion of a particular period or area in the history of the Greeks; they are words which could be said to anyone whom the speaker wished to treat generously, safe in the assurance that we cannot actually *know* whether or not a given event results from a god's intentions. In the same way, if one provokes a quarrel and then patches it up - as Agamemnon does in resolving his quarrel (*Iliad* xix) with Achilles - by claiming that his wits had been disturbed by a malign supernatural force, it is not theological reasoning that secures acceptance of such a plea, but the desire on both sides to stop quarrelling.

More than forty years before *Trojan Women*, Aeschylus had made the chorus of Argive elders in his *Agamemnon* allude to the grief and resentment excited on the Greek mainland by the arrival, year after year, of urns containing the ashes of good men killed in the fighting at Troy and cremated there, "through another man's wife". In the Athenian democracy it was possible for people to decide that such-and-such an issue was "not worth a war" - as indeed some of them did say in 431 when Sparta had declared "If you repeal the Megarian Decree, there will be no war". It looks as if Aeschylus imagines his chorus as wondering "Is it really worth a *war*, is it worth *our lives*, to get back Menelaus's wife?" Herodotus, in his curious introductory passage which purports to trace enmity between Europe and Asia back into the heroic age, attributes to the Persians the forthright view that although it is undoubtedly a crime to abduct women it is foolish and irresponsible to take great trouble to get them back; "after all, if they themselves had not been willing, they would not have been abducted" - a plea to which rapists throughout the ages have had recourse.

Perhaps some such sentiment underlies Herodotus's treatment of a famous alternative myth datable at latest to the first half of the sixth century BC. According to that version, Helen did not go to Troy at all;

Paris abducted her from Sparta, but on the voyage to Troy they encountered a storm which drove their ship to Egypt. There Helen stayed while Paris completed the voyage to Troy; the gods created a phantom in her likeness, which everyone in Troy accepted as being Helen, until the city fell, whereupon the phantom vanished and Menelaus retrieved the real Helen from Egypt on his way home. That alternative myth was actually adopted by Euripides in his *Helen*, two years after *Trojan Women*. Herodotus professes to have learned from "the priests" that Helen stayed in Egypt, but he cannot accept the idea of the phantom, because, he says, when Menelaus demanded Helen back the Trojans simply and rightly denied that they had her. And whether they had Helen herself or a convincing phantom, Priam would never have been so foolish as to imperil his family, his subjects, and the very stones of his city, just so that Paris could enjoy life with Helen. But since the Greeks did not believe his denial, they embarked on the war which lasted ten years and ended with the city's total destruction. It is striking that Herodotus does not question the reality of Helen, Paris, Priam and the Trojan War, while making no explicit criticism of Homer for falsifying history on purely artistic grounds (the story that Helen was in Troy was "better suited to epic poetry").

So far as Euripides' play goes, we can say that the answer to the question, "Who should bear the blame for the horrors exhibited in *Trojan Women*?" is multiple: Paris, for abducting Helen; Helen, for failing to resist the temptation to leave her husband and children for the enchantingly handsome Paris; Priam, for condoning Paris's behaviour; the people of Troy, for passive acceptance of Priam's tolerance; and not least, the Greek commanders, for thinking that recapturing the adulterous wife of one of their kings was worth a war.

The prologue of the play is spoken, as commonly, by a god, Poseidon, and it becomes a dialogue when Athena arrives. Poseidon speaks of Hera and Athena as having "joined in the destruction of Troy (i.e. shared responsibility with the Greeks or joined with each other?)", and to that extent he endorses Priam's consoling words to Helen. Nothing from Poseidon, though, about the Judgement of Paris, which plays so prominent a part in Helen's apologia and is rejected as an absurd story by Hecuba. Instead, we hear of the terrible storm which will fall upon the Greeks' homeward voyage, a punishment for the rape of Cassandra by Ajax in the temple of Athena. Poseidon closes the scene with three sombre verses: "Foolish is the mortal who sacks cities and their temples and tombs ... In after time, he himself perishes".

The First World War engendered in many of its participants a strong feeling that the vast, atrocious suffering which it entailed could not possibly be justified by achievement of any of the purposes with which governments embarked upon it. The "futility of war" thus established itself as a cliché which has endured to this day, even though more recent events have shown how few human actions can be less futile than armed resistance to the threat of extermination. Trojan resistance was not "futile", though unsuccessful, but for the Greeks, and above all for Agamemnon and his family, the consequences of the war were catastrophic.

A few months before *Trojan Women* was put on, the island of Melos was captured by its Athenian besiegers, who had needed reinforcement and had been the victim of spirited sallies by the besieged. The Athenians, angered by the stubbornness of the Melians, put all the adult males of Melos to death and enslaved all the women and children. It is hard to believe that the fate of Melos did not even flicker in the minds of Euripides' audience, some of whom will have known what it feels like to inflict a fatal stab on a long succession of bound captive men. Understandably impressed by the "Melian Dialogue" in which Thucydides portrayed the original negotiations between representatives of Melos and peculiarly cynical and amoral envoys from Athens, modern readers have tended to imagine that the treatment of Melos was a new departure for Athens, and indeed for the Greek world. That impression is quite false, for Athens had treated Skione in just the same way five years before Melos, and Sparta Hysiai one year before; nevertheless, the modern idea that *Trojan Women* embodies criticism of Athenian cruelty at Melos still lives. We know - as obviously Euripides could not know - that ten years after the play, when Athens had been decisively defeated, the Athenians feared that they would be treated as they had treated Melos and Skione; the attitude of Thebes gave them grounds for that fear. There were two important differences between the fall of Melos and the fall of Troy. The Melians were Greeks, but the Trojans were Phrygians, and although racial, linguistic and cultural differences between Greeks and Trojans are not apparent in Homer, by Euripides' time they could be imagined and exploited, as they are conspicuously in his *Orestes*. The other important difference is that the "sacker of cities" in Poseidon's warning is taken to have destroyed temples, sanctuaries and ancestral tombs - unlikely in the case of Melos, because the Athenians colonised the site after disposing of its native population, and gross provocation of gods and ancestral spirits is an unpromising start for a colony.

The chorus in *Agamemnon* declare their preference for a prosperity "which does not incur resentment"; they do not wish to be a "sacker of cities" (*ptoliporthes*) any more than they wish to be defeated and "in the power of another", for "the gods have their eye on those who have slaughtered many", those whose arrogance in victory leads them into violation of divine and human law. *Trojan Women* displays the slaughter, and we are left to wonder whether for the Greeks it was worth it.

Women's Voices, Women's Hands

Ruth Hazel

I would guess that if one asked someone who knew nothing about Greek tragedy what they imagined it was like, they would come up with something like "a lot of wailing women dressed in sheets". Indeed, in his film *Mighty Aphrodite* (1995), Woody Allen used exactly this kind of stereotypical preconception about ancient drama to excellent comic effect. *Trojan Women* is perhaps the Greek tragedy which, more than any other, invites such a simplistic response: it has no real story, and simply shows the responses of a number of different women who, at the fall of Troy to the Greek forces, are facing lives of slavery - destitute, bereft of their menfolk, and forcibly parted from their families. The horror of being in that situation - whether one is a man or a woman - is so great that we have to find a way to deal with it. If we identified fully with the countless victims of war, pogroms, and ethnic cleansing over the millennia, we should not be able to go on living. We would be consumed with anger and hatred against the victors, or we would be incapacitated through a sense of guilt, or we would take a misanthropic, nihilistic view of a species which could inflict such suffering on fellow creatures.

So what can we do? We can block it all out - make a sick joke about it; refuse to believe such things happen - or, if we have to recognise that they do, say that there must be some reason for it - those people must have deserved what happened to them, and are being punished by God(s), maybe; or perhaps the explanation lies in the realm of determinist causality.

However, all those responses would show us as being less humane, less willing to admit how vulnerable we are, and how much we fear suffering those terrible things we refuse directly to contemplate. One of the purposes of theatre, I would contest - and now, no less than in the fifth century BC - is to help us to confront horrors and survive with our humanity intact. Indeed, as Aristotle said in his description of theatre in the fourth century (in *Poetics*), tragedy exercises and exorcises terror and pity.

Tolstoy's novel of 1877, *Anna Karenina* (another treatment of the theme of the tragic woman, but in a different genre), opens with the statement: 'All happy families are alike, but an unhappy family is unhappy after its own fashion'. We don't need to spell out or diagnose happiness; it just is, and very grateful we are for it when it happens to us. But we do need to diagnose and identify unhappiness, in order to cope with it - even, to prevent it recurring or continuing. I think that in *Trojan Women*, Euripides presents us with a very considerable range of kinds of grief (rather more than just unhappiness, of

course).   He does this by distinguishing
between all those wailing women, and giving
them all - even, you may feel, the individual
choruswomen - an individual 'voice'.

Finding the right words

Before I look at these different voices, I want
to make a point about the process of
translation - more particularly, because David
Stuttard provides new translations for each
of the Actors of Dionysus productions, so
what follows is something he will have had to
grapple with.   Shirley A. Barlow in the
'Translator's Note' to her 1986 edition of
Trojan Women notes the difficulty of trying to
find English equivalents for the range of
Greek words for the emotions of grief. She
lists 17 different verbs describing the feeling
and utterance of lament, and remarks that if
one looks them up in a dictionary, the same
English words are given again and again to
translate them.   Moreover, these English
words ('bewail', 'lament', 'bemoan', 'cry')
have an archaic sound. "Many words which
in Victorian times did justice to the emotion of
grief [...] now sound old-fashioned" (Barlow,
1986, 37).   Similarly, how can we translate
Greek exclamations of grief such as *oimoi,
aiai, pheu, e e, ototoi*?   "Oh!" is too weak,
"Alas" is Shakespearean, and "Oh woe!" is
just ridiculous.   Modern equivalents would
probably involve blasphemies or obscenities,
and while some writers of versions of the
play have employed obscenities for the
cursing of Helen (for example, Brendan
Kennelly, in his *The Trojan Women*, 1993),

blasphemy for us, now, has to be Christian ("Christ!" "Jesus!"), which would be anachronistic if we are trying to keep to the Trojan setting.

The very process, then, of putting English language expressions of grief or suffering into the mouths of Trojan women is problematic.

<u>Not just "a lot of wailing women"</u>

First, the play's title. Is *Troiades* best translated as 'Trojan Women' or as 'Women of Troy', or even as 'Women from Troy' (which would include Helen the Spartan)? And should one insert a definite article, to differentiate '<u>The</u> Trojan Women' from some/all/any old Trojan women? It seems a minor matter, but it is one of those things which a director has to make a policy decision on for publicity material. On the analogy of another of Euripides' plays, *Phoenissiae* (Phoenician Women), "Trojan Women" puts emphasis on the women of the Chorus as a group, rather than on them as individuals, and perhaps directed its original audience to focus on what it is to be a <u>Trojan</u> - rather than a fifth-century Greek, or, even, a Melian Greek - woman. (The ethnic cleansing at Melos in 416 and the enslavement of its women and children would seem to have been in Euripides' mind when he composed his trilogy on the Trojan war for the Great Dionysia of 415.)

So, does the Chorus speak with one voice,

and in staging the play, should the director cast a set of fifteen physically matching women (or men dressed as women) and dress them in near-identical costumes?

The answer, surely, is in the way Euripides brings his Chorus on. They don't enter in perfect formation singing a well-rehearsed *parodos* (entry song) but they come on in two groups, engaging Hecuba in anxious questions. Their references to having come from indoors (154/5), and from "the tents of Agamemnon" (176/7) suggest that, atypically for a Chorus, they might have entered, not from the two side entrances to the orchestra, but from the dominating central doorway of the skene - whence they would have to make their way, past Hecuba, down into the orchestra. It is the sort of realistic, deliberately unconventional Chorus entry which would be characteristic of Euripides, the radical playwright. The split Chorus entry allows a modern director to highlight the fact that these women are not a homogenous group, and to show them as individuals expressing different experiences of grief, loss, fear and anger. This Chorus should not be dismissed as "a lot of wailing women".

Hecuba's summoning of the women, at lines 143-5, prepared us to see a cross-section of Trojan female society - the widows or mothers of Trojan warriors, and the unmarried girls, or those newly married only to be rapidly divorced by death. Hecuba addresses them as a group as "my child" (because, as queen, she is the mother of her people), but this does not exclude the possibility of casting the Chorus in line with the stereotypes of "Women" which are represented in the major speaking roles: the Virgin (Cassandra), the Wife (Andromache), the Mother (Andromache and Hecuba), and the Crone, or old woman (Hecuba). The one stereotype which probably should not feature in the Chorus is that represented by Helen: the Whore. What intensifies the pain of the Trojan women, and what, incidentally, would have helped an Athenian (even if predominantly male) audience to empathise with them, is that, although to Greek eyes foreign, these women share with Athenian citizen women a respectability and a certain status in their society. As the Chorus and the main characters keep reminding us, these women were not born to slavery, have not deserved it, and simply cannot think how they are to cope with it. The parallels with the enslaved women of Melos - some of whom might by this time have been working in Athenian households - would have been striking. There is strong argument for presenting a Chorus of women who are well-dressed, not in rags; their very unsuitedness to a life of slavery is then signalled by their appearance.

I listed, above, various female stereotypes: virgin, wife & mother, crone, and whore. However, to say that stereotypes are recognisable in the play is not to say that the characters are two-dimensional or lacking in complexity. Indeed, each of the main female roles can be seen to be slightly ambiguous;

to confound an audience's expectations to
an extent.

Hecuba

In the Prologue section, Poseidon presents
Hecuba as a kind of living exemplification of
Troy: prostrate, degraded, manifesting the
signs of mourning - tears, shorn hair. It is
significant that Hecuba refers to herself in
her first speech as a ship; she is, indeed, all
that remains of the Trojan ship of state. (She
reprises this image of herself as trying to
save the ship of state at lines 686-96.) The
ship is now disabled, deserted, it seems,
even by the god of the sea, Poseidon.
Hecuba's initial resolution is, as it were, to go
with the flow, since nothing she can do will
alter her fate. As a queen, she retains a
responsibility for her women - all that is left of
her people - and hence she calls them in to
her, to gain a kind of spurious solidarity in
grief.

An audience might expect that as Queen and
Old Woman, Hecuba's key attributes would
be nobility and endurance, and that, as
audience, it would be asked to sympathise
wholeheartedly with her because of her
noble endurance of her tragic fate. However,
Euripides' Athenian audience might have
been expecting a barbaric excessiveness of
grief, since this is, after all, a non-Greek
enemy queen (albeit of about half a
millennium before their time). Neither of
these simplifications applies. Certainly
Hecuba gives vent to extreme expressions of

grief, fury, and personal hatred, but she also exhibits what we might call female heroism in her acceptance of all that life, the Greeks and the gods can throw at her. She combines, then, what one might describe as "Athenian" and "female barbarian" traits. In addition, as we see her in dialogue with Cassandra, Andromache and Helen, we recognise psychologically realistic sketches of the mother of a daughter with mental problems, the mother-in-law (both loving and antagonistic), and the doting grandmother of a reincarnation of her favourite son.

What makes the role so interesting to play are the complexities of her character, and the twists and turns of her mind as she lives through this period of "shipwreck" - to use her own image of herself.

While trying to maintain her identity as queen, Hecuba also exhibits the concerns and responses of an ordinary woman. When Cassandra is called out into public view, Hecuba gently takes from her the marriage torch she carries, reflecting how far from her original hopes for the girl her fate - concubine to Agamemnon - will be. She returns to this idea in her speech after Cassandra's exit; what an irony it is that she took such care with the upbringing of her daughters, only to have made them more vulnerable to rape or sacrifice.

The challenge of this role is that it seems to invite full-throttle playing throughout, whereas in fact it needs very careful changes of gear. If Hecuba oversimplifies her grief in the first passages of the play, and comes in at too high a level of distraction, she will have a problem varying her pace. She has to save a good deal of emotional energy and spontaneous response for the attack on Helen, and the reception of Astyanax's body. Moreover, we should not forget that, although she attempts suicide (by hurling herself into the burning city), she is made to live on and accept slavery. Her final words are not about the past or the present, but about the future: "forward into slavery!", and they are addressed to her women as much as to herself. As a queen should, she takes the lead.

Cassandra

The role of Cassandra is another one which seems as if it could be an unrelieved rant of madness. She enters whirling torches and singing a hymn to Hymen in a terrible parody of a wedding celebration. Hecuba and the Chorus attempt to restrain her, and, of course, do not understand her, but the audience knows very well what she means by her claim that, although she may be mad, in claiming that the Trojans are actually more blessed than the Greeks, she speaks the perfect, sane truth. What she is celebrating is her part in avenging her fellow Trojans; she will be instrumental in bringing about the death of Agamemnon and the fall of the house of Atreus.

As she proceeds to make the case that the

Trojan dead were actually more fortunate than their Greek counterparts (who did not have the company of their families and friends right up to their last day, and had no loving hands to lay them out and bury them), we should remind ourselves that Euripides may be putting into the mouth of his mad prophetess the anti-war argument which was in train during the winter of 416/5, and which was finally overcome when the first expedition to Sicily was mounted in 415.

Cassandra's final speech (424-61) starts with a coolly appraising put-down of Talthybius, the Greek negotiator-herald, and then foretells the fate of the returning Greeks. From being the rather pathetic, deranged girl she seemed at her entry, she has become an authoritative voice of the God, and a reminder to the audience of the deal struck between Athene and Poseidon in the prologue section.

Andromache, the good wife

From a modern standpoint it is possible to view Andromache as a kind of Trojan Stepford Wife: she always knew, she says, when it was right for her to have her way and when it was right to defer to Hector, and kept, before her husband, "a quiet tongue and a tranquil look" (654). She didn't stray outside the home or open her doors to scandal-mongering female friends, but occupied herself with work proper to women, aiming to gain the highest reputation for being the ideal wife and mother. Without Hector, around whom her very existence had centred, she is nothing. A feminist might say that Andromache was a construct of a male society (whether mythical Trojan or fifth-century Athenian), and in the statement of her intentions, expresses the male fantasy of the perfect wife.

There are some slightly odd notes sounded in this episode, however. Andromache's entry on a Greek chariot is a kind of parody of a triumphal progress. She has Astyanax on her lap, and sits amid the weapons of her husband, so she is, quite literally, a trophy wife.

She joins in a duet of lamentation with Hecuba, but it is she who has to break to the old woman the news that her daughter, Polyxena, has been sacrificed. Although Andromache has done her best to give Polyxena the rites of burial - covering the girl's body with her own garments, and beating her breast in mourning - she voices what seems a rather heartless opinion; namely, that Polyxena is actually better off than Andromache, who has to go on living, without hope.

It is perhaps to try to give her some incentive to live that Hecuba instructs Andromache to make herself agreeable to her new master. If she does this, Hecuba says, she may be able to rear Hector's son to take revenge, at some later stage, for his father's death. Is this, also, what the good wife must have - absolution from her dead husband's surviving kin for betraying him by sleeping with his conqueror? We might wonder why suicide is not an option for her, as Hecuba suggests at 1012-14 that it would have been for Helen. We might also pause over Andromache's supposition at lines 657-60 that the fame of her excellence had reached the Greek camp, and that was what made Neoptolemus, Achilles' son, want to possess her. Is there a touch of vanity, or self-congratulation there?

When all hope is taken from Andromache, with the removal of her child, she dwindles to a trophy again, and is carried from the stage, leaving Hecuba to embody the grieving mother when Astyanax's corpse is brought in. Hecuba grieves for her grandson and her son at the same time; a joining of father and son in death which is symbolised by the laying out of Astyanax in Hector's shield.

The question of Helen

Trojan Women is just one of many works - prose fiction, rhetoric, drama - which incorporated a discussion of the character and behaviour of Helen. The crucial question was: "Was she raped or did she go willingly with Paris to Troy?" If the former, then clearly the Greeks were fighting a righteous war in the cause of honour, but if the latter, then the war was over a worthless slut, and however beautiful she might be, this did not justify the loss of life on both sides which the war incurred.

When you examine Helen's self-defence, it has the ring of realism. She doesn't pretend that she was raped - the Trojan women could bear witness to her infatuation for Paris while she was in Troy. No, she blames everything on Aphrodite, who offered her as a prize for Paris for judging the celestial beauty contest, and then threw her spell over Helen and Paris so that neither could have done otherwise than they did. In fact, Helen blames Hecuba, her chief accuser, for not having killed Paris at birth, since the omens predicted that he would be the firebrand which would destroy Troy. Then, she sets out a secondary defence case against the possible charge that after Paris's death she did not try to escape from Troy. She could produce witnesses from the guardtowers, she says, to attest to the fact that more than once they had caught her trying to escape.

The response of the Chorus women and Hecuba is that they see through her specious arguments and see her for what she is - a woman who, even in the chaos and terror of the fall of the city, had found time to check her hair and find a nice frock. Hecuba entreats Menelaus not to travel home in the same ship as Helen since just being in her company is likely to seduce him back to believing her lies. From Cassandra, from Andromache, from Hecuba and from the Chorus women, we have heard the same story: that Helen is the Great Whore, the killer of men, the shame of her sex.

In performance, one might expect, this

character would come in for stereo-typical treatment. The semiotics of dress could point her out as all that the Trojan women (and the Greek men) say she is: a scarlet woman (red dress); sex-crazed (strappy stiletto sandals, lots of cleavage); meretricious (gold jewellery); calculating and manipulative (carefully dressed hair, perhaps, or varnished nails). This would be a stereotypical, and essentially male chauvinist, view of her. But what if a director wanted to suggest that Helen *might* have a case?

One of the paradoxes of the history of performance of Greek tragedy is that plays originally written and acted by men (and perhaps watched by a solely male audience) are now being performed and consumed by women. A consequence is that some of the unsettling aspects of (particularly) Euripides' plays - aspects unsettling because they deal with the nature and behaviour of women in male-dominated societies - are brought out in performance. The example I have in mind here is from the 1995 Royal National Theatre production of *Women of Troy*, directed by Annie Castledine and Annabel Arden, with design by Iona McLeish.

In this production, before her entry cue, Helen could be seen teetering down an upstage spiral staircase in a white chiffon dress in the style made famous by Marilyn Monroe in the 1955 film, *The Seven Year Itch*. In addition to the visual cues of the white dress, high-heeled sandals and blond wig, the decision to play the Greeks as Americans, and the Spartans as Southerners, meant that Janie Dee, as Helen, could deliver her lines in a breathy Monroe lilt. By this time Monroe's association with the Kennedy brothers was well-known, and biographers had hypothesised about her life and the circumstances of her death. The message from this presentation of Helen was that she was the victim, not so much of Aphrodite, as of Aphrodite-in-the-minds-of-men. Like Monroe, Helen might be seen as an innocent victim, even when guilty of sexual misdemeanours.

A feminist take on Helen's situation could be that she was the victim of male society which makes a sexually desirable woman an object both of adoration and of exploitation. Was not Andromache the Good Wife also "constructed" in line with male expectations? A production which tries to present this view inevitably shifts the emphasis of sympathy; an audience would no longer be in total sympathy with the Trojan women, but might start to ask questions about the similarity between Trojan and Greek societies. Who are the Trojan women's real oppressors: the Greeks - or their own men? In the hands of modern women theatre practitioners, the "women" of Euripides' plays are often being given rather unexpected voices.

Women's voices, women's hands

Trojan Women is a popular Greek play for a

predominantly female institution to perform because, unlike most tragedies of the period, it offers so many acting possibilities for women. Clearly this was not a consideration for Euripides who would have been writing roles for three professional male actors to perform. (Although he might not have known until the play was written who had been chosen to act in his productions, he would have known the pool of likely candidates and may have written with particular actors in mind.) However, Euripides might be described as a proto-feminist playwright inasmuch as he appears to empower "women" (or at least, the women of myth and legend) by giving them a voice and presenting their psychological and emotional complexities through his female characters.

One of the few occasions on which it was permissible for women to raise their voices in public in fifth-century Athens was at funerals. Similarly, it was women's hands which laid out the corpses and prepared them for burial, and women's hands which performed the rituals of mourning. However, during the course of the Peloponnesian wars, the sound of female lamentation at funerals of sons, husbands, brothers, fathers killed in war could have seemed a challenge to (male) state authority. Restrictions were put on the numbers of women who might attend the ritual mourning, and you will, I'm sure, know of the famous speech by Pericles, when the first dead of the Peloponnesian war came home to Athens for burial, in which he exhorted Athenian women to show their greatness (and their solidarity with the war effort) by not being heard or seen indulging their feelings of grief.

Obviously it would be anachronistic nonsense to say that *Trojan Women* is a feminist play because that suggests the presence in 415 BC of a modern feminist consciousness. Nor have we any way of hearing the genuine voice of Athenian women from the mouths of Euripides' fictional and mythical characters. But *Trojan Women* is undoubtedly a play in which the voice of the victimised, the enslaved, the abused and the bereaved is heard, and early feminists would have said that that is a female voice. In 1919 when Sybil Thorndike played Hecuba (rather young, and with her own son playing her grandson, Astyanax), she was greeted after one performance by a working class woman with: "...them Trojans was just like us. We've lost our sons and 'usbands in this bleedin' war, 'aven't we? So no wonder we was all cryin'. That was a real play, that was, dearie". (Casson, 1972, 64)

In that woman's mind, at least, the anti-war message of the play expressed a female protest against a male-run militaristic Establishment which had sent sons, husbands, brothers, fathers to their deaths, and in that respect, had turned state-sanctioned violence against its own vulnerable members.

Feminist critics of the 1970s and 1980s

would similarly have found material in the play which struck a sympathetic note, not so much in the anti-war message, but in the depiction of women's total dependency on men - emotional, physical, institutionalised, religious - a dependency amounting, a '70s feminist would say, to subjugation, or, to use the modish word of the period, "colonisation". Such critics would argue that the Trojan women's slavery began in their days of peace and prosperity when every act of their lives was controlled by a male-run state, and they were even defined in terms of their relationships to men: "daughter of Priam", "wife of Hector", "mother of Astyanax". The play focuses on the women at a point when, paradoxically, they are in one respect at their most free, since they have not yet passed into the hands of their Greek masters and are able to express their feelings freely to women equally bereft and wretched.

What we ought to note about this view of the play is that the Trojan women are not expressing any kind of early feminist protest about male domination of women in general. There is no breath of reproach against Trojan men, or against oppressive male chauvinist societal structures of the city of Troy. Hector was great, Priam was royal, Astyanax a poppet, and even Paris, the cause of the whole war, was totally irresistible in his flashy clothes and gold jewellery. No; the Trojan women direct their anger and reproaches against the Greeks, Helen, and the gods.

Helen has already been discussed, but it is

not inappropriate to link her, the subject for the Trojan women's hatred, with the gods who are the subject of their resentment and questioning. Helen was, after all, a daughter of Zeus, and by her own assertion, a mere pawn of her goddess half-sister, Aphrodite. Are the gods, then, the real oppressors and tyrants who have brought about the destruction of Troy?

In Euripides' representations of them, the gods tend to be, not better, but worse, than humans; more extreme in their passions, and, of course, more powerful in their pursuit of the fulfilment of them. *Trojan Women* begins (as a number of Euripides' plays do) with personal appearances by the gods; in this case, Poseidon, lamenting the destruction of his own favourite city, Troy, and Athene, who, having supported the Greeks hitherto, against Aphrodite, Hera, and Poseidon, has taken serious offence at the Greeks' lack of proper respect for her temple in Troy - from the sanctuary of whose altar Cassandra was torn by Ajax. Throughout the play there are references to Pallas Athene as unfriendly to Troy, but the Trojan women do not realise what the audience does: that negotiations between the two gods will ensure that the Greeks will be heavily punished for their collective hubris.

In the third stasimon of *Trojan Women* the Chorus questions Zeus himself (1060-80): did he care at all about Troy and all those Trojans who had offered him sacrifices and worship for so long? After her lament over the mangled body of her grandson, Hecuba gives her own answer: no; the gods did not care, or if they did, it was only to care about destroying Troy. But the audience knows that the situation is almost worse than that: the gods do not greatly care either way about humans in general (although they may favour individuals, as Aphrodite did Paris); the gods only care about themselves. This is the message which Euripides gives his audience, but which he spares Hecuba from knowing. Hecuba finds some consolation for the hatred of the Gods in the belief that Troy will live on in legend <u>because</u> of its sufferings (lines 1240-45). Troy's death throes and the grief of the Trojan women will become famous through the songs of future poets.

In a number of ways, then, we may see Euripides himself as giving in *Trojan Women* a voice to an alien force; a voice which was subversive in its 'pro-otherness'. He seems to be asking for the audience's sympathy for the Trojan women, but concealed in the narrative of legend are questions about the ethics of waging war on racially similar peoples; about the treatment of war victims; about the existence and nature of the gods. Such dangerously subversive ideas could only be expressed with impunity, even in the context of theatre, in an ancient and far-away world, and by the voices and gestures of foreign women.

Melos and the *Trojan Women*

Keith Sidwell

The *Trojan Women* was produced as part of a trilogy at the Dionysia festival of spring 416/415 BC. It dramatises sympathetically (so it seems) the appalling suffering of the women of Troy as their individual fates are decided by the victorious Greek commanders and reflects harshly (as most think) upon the barbaric cruelty of the Greeks in their hour of victory. However, by the artifice of a conversation in the prologue between Poseidon, friend of Troy, and Athena, its bitterest enemy, the play's structure also ensures that the audience is aware of the punishment in store for the Greek leaders on their way home for those excesses which have given direct offence to the goddess.

The date of the play's production and its sympathetic handling of the distress of an enemy brought low by Greeks have suggested to (some) readers a connection between the plot of the drama and the events on the island of Melos in the winter immediately preceding, as related by Thucydides in this brief coda to book five of his history of the Peloponnesian War:

"About this same time [the winter of 416/415 BC] the Melians again captured another part of the Athenian lines where there were only a few of the garrison on guard. As a result of this, another force came out afterwards from Athens under the command of Philocrates, the son of Demeas. Siege operations were now carried on vigorously and, as there was also some treachery from inside, the Melians surrendered unconditionally to the Athenians, who put to death all the men of military age whom they took, and sold the women and children as slaves. Melos itself they took over for themselves, sending out later a colony of 500 men." (Thucydides, 5. 116, tr. Rex Warner)

Shirley Barlow, in the introduction to her edition of the *Trojan Women* (Warminster, 1986), writes, albeit cautiously (pp. 26-7): "...the political context of the time at which it was written seems to be significant, and to have some bearing on why it was written as it was. The Athenians' destruction of Melos had occurred in the previous year, and the enslavement of its women and children and the slaughter of its male population might have influenced Euripides in his presentation of the Trojans' predicament at the hands of the Greeks." Alan Sommerstein, referring generically to a well-known phenomenon, widens the perspective to include Athenian imperialism as a whole when he says: "Euripides' *Trojan Women* ... has often been seen as an attack on the aggressive, expansionist spirit that was soon to launch the Sicilian expedition" (*Greek Tragedy and the Historian*, ed. C. Pelling, Oxford 1997, p. 72). Robert Parker, even more circum-spectly, appears to see some generic religious message emanating from the play for its Athenian audience, presumably also in relation to their own conduct in the real world, when he writes (*Greek Tragedy and the Historian*, ed. C. Pelling, Oxford 1997, p. 155): "*Troades* does, it seems, defy civic optimism with a shocking force. Of course, the city which the love of the gods failed to defend was not Athens, but the spectator would have been complacent indeed who did not feel that it might have been."

There is a long-standing and on-going scholarly debate about the nature and function of Greek tragedy, including whether it can in any sense be called "political". In recent years, a consensus has grown up that tragedy, given that it was produced at the demos' instigation and under its control (through the archon, whose job it was to award choruses), was in some general sense concerned with civic ideology - though whether to confirm it or to subvert it is still a matter of debate - but did not, as a rule, concern itself with the specifics of contemporary history or matters of policy (see in particular "*The Great Dionysia and civic ideology*", Simon Goldhill, JHS 107 (1987), 58-76, the recent counterblast to the consensus by Jasper Griffin, "*The Social Function of Attic Tragedy*" CQ 48 (1998), 39-61 and Richard Seaford's reply to Griffin in CQ 50 (2000), 30-44). On the 'civic ideology' model, the search for references to Melos and the Sicilian expedition is chimerical: the use of myth (or even, in the case of Aeschylus' *Persians*, of recent history) as the raw material for tragic drama of itself dictates the necessary generality of the interaction between tragic plot and actuality.

Yet there are exceptions. The Persian threat was by no means at an end when Aeschylus produced his *Persians* in 472 BC (with Pericles as his choregos). The treatment of the Areopagus and the Argive alliance in his *Eumenides* of 458 BC have seemed to many far too precise (even in their heroic vagueness) to be anything but reflections of quite specific recent events. In the *Trojan Women* itself, Sommerstein's comment already quoted is made in the context of the following remark: "Even in Euripides' *Trojan Women*, which has often been seen [etc. as above] ..., the chorus go out of their way to express their special loathing of the thought that they may find themselves living as slaves at Sparta of all places" (id. pp. 72-3). And Barlow links lines 220ff. from the same choral passage to the Sicilian expedition of 415 BC, because "there is a reference to Sicily by the chorus which seems to be somewhat clumsily brought into the Trojan context" (id. p. 27).

The questions I want to pose in this brief essay, are (1) what modes of interpretation by Athenians of tragic plays do the types of comment made by Barlow, Sommerstein and Parker imply, (2) is there any external evidence to support the existence of these modes among the play's original audience, and (3) is there any (ideological) interference in the minds of modern readers/audiences which might be dictating ways of understanding the play's effect?

(1) Barlow's formulation lays emphasis upon the relationship between the events on Melos and Euripides' intention in constructing the play's plot the way he did. Sommerstein's comment suggests a feeling that somehow Euripides' intention was communicated to the Athenians as a sort of message of disapproval of expansionism. Underlying both assessments is the notion that Athenians in the theatre would be looking for connections between mythical and current events and had some template ready to hand to translate their findings. Parker carefully distinguishes the message received by his audience from allegorisation (the city destroyed in the play is Troy), but nevertheless implies that they will be susceptible to general reflection about themselves as human agents in relation to the gods (which will perhaps make them more cautious in their handling of real affairs in the polis?).

Presumably, then, there was available some mindset which Euripides relied upon for the translation of the mythical material into political analysis. What it is, however, none of the commentators precisely articulates. Is Barlow thinking of allegorisation? Possibly. But any crude version will not work. Troy is not Athens (as Parker notes), the main Greek leaders are Peloponnesians, not

Athenians, the treachery which delivered Melos came from within (not successful siege operations by the Athenians, nor yet any kind of "wooden horse" strategem), and there is no indication in Thucydides that sacrilegious acts were performed by the Athenians during the town's capture. In fact, the Greeks did not colonise Troy as part of an imperialist expansion project, but utterly razed it, destroying also with Astyanax' death the possibility of its later refoundation. Melos was not only not destroyed, but, like Aegina earlier in the war, appropriated by Athenian colonists. Moreover, not all the Melian male population perished (Xenophon, *Hellenica* II, 2,9 tells us that Lysander restored the survivors at the end of the war), and a particular contrast might be drawn between the fact that in Melos only those in their prime were killed, while at Troy even old Priam was despatched. On the central issue which seems shared, the enslavement of the women, in *Trojan Women* the leaders pick out their favoured women and take them home, while in the real world of Melos, the women were sold into slavery.

Parker's image of a general disquiet which might have been engendered in the audience as they thought of themselves *qua* human beings in the thrall of those powers Herodotus described as "jealous and inclined to create trouble" is more plausible. But the demos itself, the presumed audience of tragedy, was the agent of the policy which had brought Melos to its terrible fate. Decisions of this kind were fairly normal in times of conflict (witness the Mytilene debate earlier in the Peloponnesian War) and could cause (as in that case) division of opinion and changes of mind. But in the Melos case and in that of Mytilene, the kinds of consideration that Thucydides gives to his speakers are centred around the use of (enlightened) self-interest in the formulation of political policy. Specifically on the religious issue, in fact, when the Melians invoke their trust in the gods' goodwill (5.104), Thucydides makes the Athenians respond thus (5.105): "So far as the favour of the gods is concerned, we think we have as much right to that as you have. Our aims and our actions are perfectly consistent with the beliefs men hold about the gods and with the principles which govern their own conduct. Our opinion of the gods and our knowledge of men lead us to conclude that it is a general and necessary law of nature to rule whatever one can... And therefore, so far as the gods are concerned, we see no good reason why we should fear to be at a disadvantage." (tr. Rex Warner). It is a moot point whether or not Thucydides as an intellectual critic of Athenian democracy was implicitly attacking the decision about Melos (I tend to think that here he is giving the ambassadors arguments of which he would approve, as an example of the Realpolitik of political negotiations), but it is worth considering just how, practically, a person could act upon the insight that human actions have unpredictable outcomes. Would it make a difference? Yes, in the case of Nicias, apparently, whose over-reliance upon superstition itself caused his death, but not in the case of Alcibiades, whose apparent disrespect for religion did not prevent his creating disastrous problems for the city whose circumspection sent him into exile.

(2) It is clear that allegorisation as a mode of thought was available in the later fifth century. We have evidence of its use in the interpretation of Homer and Hesiod well before this date. However, it seems to be a province of intellectuals (Anaxagoras among them) rather than of plain folk, though it could focus upon the decoction of moral truths from poetry. But a solid picture of Athenian modes of reception is hard to come by and has been attempted only partially and sporadically. For the fifth century, there is little evidence. The response of the Athenians to Phrynichus' *Capture of Miletus* - a fine and a ban on its future production, because it brought onto the stage "disasters close to home" (Herodotus 6.21) - suggests that a boundary between the theatrical world and the real was drawn in favour of the representation of other people's sorrows. But it is difficult to say whether this implies anything about covert political criticism, since we do not know whether or not Phrynichus was implying that Athens should have done more to help Miletus. A fragment of Gorgias suggests that fear and pity are central to an audience's reaction, and this seems like the beginning of a reader-response theory built upon in the fourth century by Aristotle in the *Poetics*. Further, the final scene of Aristophanes' *Frogs* suggests that the city's

politics are a concern to the tragic poets and that their plays may have a part in the rescue of the polis from its current dangers (1420ff.). Elsewhere in the *Frogs*, individual plays are characterised as able to have an energising or ennervating effect (1010ff.), depending upon the nobility or otherwise of the characters portrayed. Peter Wilson ("The use of tragedy in the fourth century", *Tragedy and the Tragic*, ed. M.S. Silk, Oxford, 1996, 310-331) has looked at the way fifth century tragedy is evoked by the fourth century orators and from this it is clear that the notion of tragic characters and their actions as paradigmatic existed and continued in the world outside the comic theatre. From his study we can add the out-of-context quotation of tragic lines to reinforce an ethical point, and the use of bad characters and their evil actions in tragedy to abuse an opponent in the courts.

A particularly instructive example of the latter for the present topic comes from the speech *Against Alcibiades*, ascribed to Andocides:

"After recommending that the Melians be sold into slavery, Alcibiades purchased a woman from among the captives and has had a child by her - a child whose birth is more transgressive than Aigisthos', since his parents are each other's bitterest enemies and his family is divided between those who have committed and those who have suffered the most extreme wrongs... When you watch such things in tragedies you regard them with horror, but when you see them taking place in the polis you think nothing of them..." ([Andocides] 4.22-3, tr. Wilson, pp. 319-20)

The writer makes it clear that he regards the actions taken against the Melians as wrongs (presumably not a position taken by the demos in 416/415), but his main point is to emphasise the very different reactions provoked by fictive dramatic characters and deeds and real ones. Underlying this, however, is the notion that the audience response to tragedy is correct and that the lessons taught by these paradigmatic events ought to be (but are not) transferred into the real world of the city (where they do occur).

It is clear, then, that ancient writers do envisage some sort of cause and effect between tragic drama and the world of the polis. But it does not seem to involve the direct reading of a drama onto an event so much as the perception of tragic-style patterns in events. From this perspective, it seems more likely that the audience of *Trojan Women* will participate in mourning the effects of bad actions and mistaken policies (such as those of Hecabe and Priam in raising Paris and later not forcing him to return Helen), just as seems to be the case in *Persians*. Nonetheless, it is worth remembering that Aristophanes' Aeschylus claims that in producing *Persians* he was encouraging the idea of perpetual victory over one's enemies (*Frogs* 1026-7). Whatever the precise joke is, there does seem to be a case for suggesting that the audience of *Trojan Women* might be capable of a response which involved both pity for the victims and a sense of pride in conquest (the Trojan War was later the mythical paradigm for Alexander's conquests) moderated by the fear engendered by the possibility of excess caused by bad character and bad judgement. In real life, then, Athenians might have felt pity for the victims of the Melian affair (was this in fact Alcibiades' motive for buying a captive?), but justified in their actions, alongside complete bafflement at the lack of judgement shown by the leaders of the Melians in rejecting their reasonable overtures. But since their own actions could be considered reasonable and the disaster had actually befallen the Melians, there seem to be no grounds for suspecting that they would have suddenly seen themselves and their actions at Melos in this play. At Melos, the tragedy played out was entirely Melian.

(3) Despite this, it has seemed, apparently, quite natural for modern readers and critics to think of Melos in connection with the *Trojan Women*. It is worthwhile asking why, given that the argument from ancient attitudes seems to point in other directions.

Shelley's famous formulation "We are all Greeks" in a way figures the temptation we feel to assume that because the tragic drama of the Athenians still speaks to us, it says the same things as it did to them. But there are fundamental distinctions to be made, at every level, between their experience of life and their basic assumptions about the world and our own. For one thing, we not only live in societies without slavery, but slavery itself is anathema to us. Athenians lived with slavery and, though some ancient authors criticised the institution as contrary to nature and justice, the general view even among philosophers was that it was simply a given fact of human existence. Secondly, our idea of freedom does not exist in a polarity with slavery and is thus fundamentally different from a freedom which does. Thus at a gut level, we are inclined to read the play's representation of forced enslavement against a different ideological matrix.

This inclination, I suggest, is what makes it easier for us to be influenced by the proximity in time of the Melian affair to the production of *Trojan Women*. For us, incidents involving the (cold-blooded) destruction of cities and the enslavement of its women and children are remarkable enough that a theatrical representation of such an event following so closely upon what we judge to be a real event of the same kind simply must be connected, and the theatrical representation must be in a critical relation with the real event. Unlike ourselves, however, the Athenians could make distinctions between the pity to be accorded the victims of enslavement and the iron law of power politics which justified their enslavement.

Conclusion

In this essay, I have tried to track the symptoms of our habits of reading the *Trojan Women*, and to attempt a general diagnosis, rather than write a completely rigorous account. Two important points need to be stressed. First of all, as historians of Greek culture, we are obliged in looking at a question like the relation between Melos and the Trojan Women to try to reconstruct a cognitive syntax for Athenian viewers (remembering that diverse views of the same phenomena are also going to be as much a part of their discourse as they are with us). This is difficult, because our evidence is slight and our sources are biased towards the intellectual elite who are so often critical of the very forms of dramatic representation staged by the Athenian demos. Secondly, we need to see ourselves and our own cultural assumptions and interpetative methods as part of the picture and the problem. And such assumptions and methods do not remain constant. I have not looked at the history of the association between Melos and the *Trojan Women*, but it would surely tell us something in itself of the changing pattern of our own approaches. Did societies with slaves or great empires see the same connection as we do?

That question awaits further investigation. For the moment, however, it looks as though some late twentieth century critics, though cautiously, have been inclined to accept the critical connection between Melos and the

Trojan Women as embedded in our perceptions of the play's meaning and design. My discussion challenges this acceptance. I doubt very much that Athenians would have made this connection at all, or that it was in any way intended by Euripides. The view of Athens presented in the play by the chorus is entirely favourable: it is their first choice of a location to live their lives as slaves (207-8, 218-19). And the poet was not prescient (or, like Thucydides, writing after the defeat of Athens). He could not know that the conflict with Sparta was not over and that the Sicilian expedition would lead to a disaster almost as great for Athens as was the capture of their island for the Melians. And if the inclusion of Sicily in the desirable places listed by the chorus to be a slave (220f.) is to be connected with the enthusiasm at Athens for the adventure (see Barlow's remark quoted above), then it looks rather like an authorial endorsement than anything else, just as their repugnance at Sparta looked to Sommerstein like an expression of the gut hatred still felt against that city in Athens.

So let us clear Melos from our minds also, and try to concentrate upon the play's ethical focus, especially its investigation of the tricky boundaries which mark off humane from hybristic behaviour in the human sphere and what acts are likely to earn the wrath of the divine players in this unpredicatble universe. We might also note the importance of the question of responsibility. The judgement of whose mistakes caused the debacle is the issue formally at stake in the agon between Hecabe and Helen, but it must also have been in the heads of an audience which had earlier seen Hecabe reject the gods' injunction not to raise Paris in the *Alexandros*, the first play of the "trilogy". And we must not forget, while we are thinking about this and wondering what Euripides was contributing to the demos in the realm of advice about its conduct of affairs (if the Aristophanic picture is not merely a topsy-turvy jest), that the very stuff of this tragedy, which for us is categorised as "myth", was treated by Athenians (and other Greeks) as part of their history, which could be used as argument for political action by rhetoricians in the assembly. To that extent, issues which are of little concern to us, such as the provenance of Talthybius (connected in the fifth century with the herald clan at Sparta) and Menelaus (King of Sparta), may have loomed large in the assessment of an Athenian audience embroiled not only in fighting but also in policy-making decisions about conflicts against other Greeks.

Euripides' *Trojan Women*: Relevance and Universality

Alex Garvie

Euripides' *Trojan Women* was first produced in Athens at the City Festival of the god Dionysus in the spring of 415 B.C. For sixteen years Athens had been engaged in the Peloponnesian War against Sparta and her allies. The play deals with the aftermath of the Trojan War, when, the Greeks having after ten years succeeded in capturing Troy, the Trojan men have all been killed, and the women are about to be taken off into slavery in Greece. In 416 B.C. the Athenians had attacked the Aegean island of Melos, which had hitherto remained neutral in the War, and, having massacred the male population, had enslaved the women and children of the island - an act of barbarity which had made a great impression on the historian Thucydides, who devotes considerable space to it in the fifth book of his *History of the Peloponnesian War*. It is hard to believe that this recent event was not in the mind of Euripides as he wrote the play, or in the minds of his audience as they watched it. But what were they to make of a tragedy which encourages them to sympathise with the victims when they themselves had been the conquerors?

Fifth-century Athenian comedy is unashamedly political, but fifth-century tragedy very rarely alludes directly to contemporary events. Its subject-matter is drawn almost exclusively from the world of myth, and only one surviving play is set in the centre of Athens. A few tragedies are known to have dealt with the Persian Wars, a fact which tells us more about how the Greeks regarded the defeat of the Persians, as an event of mythical proportions, than about any desire to bring tragedy into the world of every-day contemporary life. Only one of these plays has survived, the *Persians* of Aeschylus, which, first presented in 472 B.C., has as its subject the aftermath of the Battle of Salamis in 480 B.C. The historian Herodotus tells us that Phrynichus in the 490s presented a play which dealt with the capture of Miletos in the Ionian revolt against the Persians, and he was heavily fined for reminding his Athenian audience of the misfortunes of their Ionian cousins. It is unclear why the Athenians set their tragedies so firmly in the world of myth. It seems unlikely that there was any kind of formal or official ban on the choice of a contemporary theme. Probably, from the very beginning of tragedy in the sixth century, there was a feeling that myth provided the ideal embodiment for the truths that the tragedians aimed to present, stripped of everything that might seem accidental, trivial, and temporary. Indeed a long tradition of choral lyric poetry had trained the Athenians to see their own temporary concerns regularly against the unchanging and permanent background of the world of myth.

It would be wrong to think of Greek tragedy as providing a kind of escape for the audience from the concerns of "real life". The plays were produced at the City Festival of Dionysus, the other events of which were undoubtedly political in their implication. It was on this occasion, for example, that war-orphans were paraded in the theatre and took an oath to fight on behalf of the city, that honours were bestowed on meritorious citizens, and that the tribute from Athens' allies was brought into the theatre. A large part of the audience must have consisted of the same men as sat and voted in the democratic Assembly. Many scholars therefore feel that the presentation of tragedies must somehow have had a part to play in this, and have tried in various ways to relate each tragedy to the particular political concerns of the original audience at the time of its first production, and more generally to what is often described as "democratic civic ideology". A few years ago the tendency was to search for specific allusions to contemporary events, and to treat each tragedy as if it were a kind of political allegory, often with the principal mythical characters "standing for" various leading Athenian statesmen. So Zeus in *Prometheus Bound* could be seen as representing Pericles. More recently the process has become less crude and more sophisticated, but current orthodoxy continues to stress the need to examine each play in the context of its first production, to ask what the playwright was saying to, or even trying to teach, his original audience.

Conversely, there is perhaps at present less stress on the universality of Greek tragedy. Indeed, the very notion of universality is sometimes derided as a sentimental relic of the Romantic Age. And yet many modern audiences, or readers, of Greek tragedies would, despite the scholars, claim that they have something to say to them, and that in our own day it is not only to those who are versed in the intricacies of fifth-century Athenian politics that they make sense. Further difficulties arise when we try to determine more precisely the position of the tragedians *vis-à-vis* this democratic civic ideology. For some scholars the playwright's job is to confirm and reinforce it, so that if he sets his play in some other city, such as Thebes, that is because it allows him to demonstrate the catastrophes that strike a city which is not governed by an ideal democracy. For others the tragedian sets out to question, and even to subvert, the conventional notions of democracy. It seems best to conclude that the relationship between the spectator and the tragic character, who is regularly distanced from him by time and/or by space, is a complex one. It is a mistake, too, to suppose that all the spectators would react in the same way to the theatrical experience. It is not always easy to grasp the playwright's purpose, but the best way to start is to examine the clues provided by the construction of his plot, and the way in which its themes are presented and developed.

How, then, did the original audience of *Trojan*

Women react to a play that presented the sufferings of war from the point of view of the victims, the sufferings which they themselves had inflicted on the people of Melos only a year earlier? It is hard to deny that some at least must have felt uncomfortable, and that this was Euripides' intention. Certainly a long tradition of epic poetry had accustomed a fifth-century Greek audience to sympathise with the Trojans as well as with the Greek warriors at Troy. Homer's *Iliad* may be concerned primarily with the tragedy of the Greek hero Achilles, but in the background, and sometimes even in the foreground, is the suffering of war as it affects both sides. Homer is no Greek chauvinist. Indeed it is the death of the Trojan champion, Hector, at the hands of Achilles in Book 22 that provides the climax of the poem, and the mourning of his family receives extensive treatment. His death is movingly foreshadowed as early as Book 6, when his wife, Andromache, begs him in vain to remain in safety inside the city, and then says good-bye to him for what Homer's audience must have known would be the last time. Throughout the poem the inevitable fall and destruction of the city are also clearly foreshadowed. Andromache knows that one day she will be taken off into slavery by the victorious Greeks. It is with the funeral of Hector that the poem ends, and not with any sense of triumph in the knowledge that the Greeks will shortly defeat their enemies.

What is remarkable, then, about Euripides' play is not simply that he presents the suffering of the Trojan War from the point of view of the Trojan victims, but that he does so at a time when the sufferings that the Athenians themselves had inflicted on the Melians were still so fresh in their minds. The story of the Trojan War was hallowed by tradition, but the harsh realities of their own experience were quite another matter. For a parallel we have to look to Aeschylus' *Persians*, produced, as we have seen, in 472 B.C., only eight years after the Battle of Salamis, in which they themselves had played a major role in defeating the Persian enemy, and in saving the Greek world from the domination of the barbarian Persians. In the earlier Persian invasion under Darius Aeschylus himself fought at Marathon, a battle in which his brother was killed, and he probably took part at Salamis, so that his account in Persians is the earliest surviving eyewitness account of that battle. In 472 the Persians were still a threat, and to fifth-century democratic freedom-loving Athenians they stood for all that they most despised in oriental despotism and decadence. For them the Persians were par excellence "the Other". One might, therefore, expect Aeschylus' play to be a celebration of the decisive victory of Salamis, and that, indeed, is exactly what some modern scholars have taken it to be. Gilbert Murray even thought that it might have been part of a regular celebration of the victory in Athens in the 470s. Others have seen it as a kind of satire on the ways of oriental monarchs, with the audience laughing uproariously at the sight of the defeated king

Xerxes who appears in rags at the end of the play. There is, however, a danger that, if we approach a play by means of the context in which it was produced, we may read into it, and easily persuade ourselves that we have found, what is not actually there. Many attempts have been made recently to define what is meant by saying that tragedy is usually "tragic". It is hard, however, to see how a patriotic celebration could fit into any satisfactory definition of the term.

Of course Aeschylus was glad that the Greeks had defeated the Persians, and there are undoubtedly patriotic touches in the play. One may think of the dialogue between Atossa, Xerxes' mother, and the Chorus-leader, in which the former enquires about far-off Athens, and the nature of its military forces and its government. The Chorus-leader tells her (line 242) that "they are called the slaves and subjects of no man", and she cannot understand how such a people could resist an invading army. The audience would certainly enjoy this praise of the Athenian democratic system. Even more would they relish the description of the cry of the Greeks as they went into battle: "Advance, you sons of the Greeks, set free your fatherland, set free your children, wives, the shrines of your ancestral gods, and the tombs of your ancestors; now is the struggle on behalf of all" (402-5). Many critics, however, have been struck by the fact that such passages are so few. Aeschylus contrives to make us see the tragedy almost entirely through the eyes of the defeated Persians. We may expect a celebration, but it is not what we receive. The play is set, not in Greece, but in distant Susa, the capital of the Persian empire. Not a single Greek is named, whereas we are given three long catalogues of Persian names, one at the beginning as the Chorus describes the men who went off full of confidence to battle, one in the middle where we hear from the Messenger of the deaths of the noblest of the Persians, and one in the closing scene in which Xerxes and the Chorus together lament the dead. As they leave the stage language almost breaks down altogether and turns into inarticulate cries. The victims are not set up for the audience to laugh at, but appear as brave men who did not deserve to die. This is not a celebration but a tragedy, the tragedy of both Xerxes and his people, the story of a fall, through *hamartia* or error, from prosperity and success to utter ruin - the best kind of tragedy according to Aristotle in his *Poetics*. Aeschylus encourages his audience to consider the reasons for the Persians' fall, but, despite many critics, he provides no easy answers. It seems likely that the audience leaves the theatre, not crowing over a beaten enemy, nor confident in the future, but uneasily aware that they too could one day be the victims of such a fall. For the Athenians the Persians may be "the Other", but they are also fellow-human beings, and it is in "the Other" that they see themselves. A few years earlier, perhaps in 476 B.C. Phrynichus had presented a play, *Phoenician Women*, on the same subject. Unfortunately we do not know enough about

it to tell whether his treatment was the same
as that of Aeschylus, but the title, derived
from the Chorus which consisted of the wives
of the Phoenician allies of the Persians,
suggests that it may have been not so very
different.

Euripides too in his *Trojan Women* presents
the aftermath of the sack of a city in such a
way that we sympathise, not with the triumph
of the victors, but with the victims in their
sufferings.   He directs his audience's
response at the very beginning of the play,
when the god Poseidon, in the opening
speech of the Prologue, says farewell to the
city of Troy, which, as he says, he has loved
constantly ever since he and Apollo built its
walls. In the *Iliad* Poseidon was on the side
of the Greeks, but Euripides has turned him
into a supporter of Troy. Athena enters, the
traditional supporter of the Greeks, and the
patron-goddess   in   particular   of   the
Athenians, who have so recently sacked the
Island of Melos. Yet she too asserts that she
wishes to comfort the Trojans who were
formerly her enemies, and to give the
Achaean army a bitter return home (65-6).
She is angry because Ajax, son of Oileus,
has dragged the Trojan princess Cassandra
from her shrine. The play, then, begins with
divine sympathy for the Trojans and hostility
towards the Greeks, and Euripides is surely
inviting his audience to share these feelings.
The only Greek commander whom we shall
meet on stage is the weak and unimpressive
Menelaus, who enters at line 860, rejoicing
that he will now be able to kill Helen in

revenge for leaving him with Paris, but who, after listening to the debate between Hecuba and Helen, ineffectually puts off the execution until he has got her home to Sparta. Contrast the heroic picture that we are given of the Trojan Hector who died bravely fighting for his country. Even the Greek Talthybius describes him as *aristos*, "excellent", the highest term of commendation (709, 723). Odysseus, although we do not meet him, is always there in the background, the principal source of misery for the Trojan women. As often, but not always, in tragedy he is portrayed as a deceitful, unscrupulous villain, or at least that is the impression that we are given by the, admittedly biased, women: see for example Hecuba's description of him at 282-7, when she learns that she is to become his slave; and her words at 1224-5. It is Odysseus who persuades the Greek assembly that the little boy Astyanax, Hector's son, should be killed, thrown down from the city-walls, in case he should grow up to be as great as his father. Hecuba at 1190-1 imagines his epitaph: "the Greeks once killed this child because they were afraid of him"; and she adds that this will be a "shameful epitaph for Greece". Andromache too, Hector's widow and the mother of Astyanax, when she hears of her son's impending fate, reviles the Greeks, as "having devised crimes fit for barbarians" (*barbara kaka* 764). Yet Euripides' audience despised barbarians, and prided itself on its civilised values. One may compare his *Medea*, produced in 431 B.C., in which for most of the play Euripides contrives to engage his audience's sympathy on the side of Medea, a barbarian and a woman, against the despicable Jason, a Greek and a man.

It is with the Trojans, then, rather than the Greeks that Euripides makes his Greek audience sympathise. But it is not a matter of black and white. The role of Talthybius, the Greek herald, is to bring to the Trojan women news of the offstage decisions and events. On his first appearance he reports on the allocation of the women to their conquerors. Agamemnon is to receive Cassandra as his concubine, while Polyxena, daughter of Hecuba is to attend the tomb of Achilles. The audience, but not Hecuba, understands the irony. It has already heard from Poseidon in the Prologue that Polyxena has been sacrificed at the tomb. Hecuba will learn it only later. Andromache is to go with Neoptolemus, the son of Achilles, and Hecuba with Odysseus. It is on his second appearance that Talthybius announces the coming death of Astyanax. At first somewhat brusque in manner, Talthybius himself gradually becomes more sympathetic to the women. On his second entrance he begins (709-11) by begging Hecuba not to hate him, because it is not of his own will that he brings the news about Astyanax. At 717 he says, "I do not know how to tell you easily of your misfortunes"; and at 786-9, "Such things should be announced by someone who is pitiless and more a friend to shamelessness than is my mind". On his third appearance it is with expressions of genuine pity that he describes the child's death, and describes how he himself has washed the body and is preparing to assist Hecuba with the funeral (1151-5) - tasks which would normally belong to the family. Greek victor and Trojan victim are united in a common grief and a sense of shared humanity.

There are, moreover, hints of coming tragedy for the victorious Greeks themselves. In the Prologue Poseidon and Athena plan together to wreck the Greek fleet on its homeward voyage, and Poseidon remarks (95-7) that the man who sacks cities, temples, and tombs is a fool and that he later perishes himself. In her speech at 353 ff. the prophetess Cassandra predicts the death of Agamemnon, the Greek commander-in-chief, on his return home to Greece, and the ruin of all his house. She even argues (365-6) that in a very real sense Troy is more blessed than Greece: the Trojans have the finest glory, in that they died fighting for their country, while it is through his death that Hector's reputation as a hero has been secured. Odysseus too is to suffer on his homeward journey (430 ff.). There is then for the audience a bitter irony in Talthybius' words at 1263-4: "so that, having sacked the city of Troy, we may set out gladly from Troy for home". The notion that success cannot last is prominent in Greek thought from Homer onwards. Hecuba has fallen from prosperity to ruin. By the end of the play we know that there will be no happiness for either victim or victor. Helen, it is true, will escape execution, and the audience knows from the *Odyssey* that Menelaus will not in fact kill her when they return to Sparta. The only major character who can look forward to a happy future is the one who caused the War which has ruined so many innocent people on both sides. It all seems so unfair. As they think of Melos Euripides' spectators are certainly not encouraged to look to the future with confidence. In Euripides' later plays, as in late fifth-century thought in general, the concept of *tyche*, chance, becomes increasingly frequent - the idea that life is haphazard and unpredictable, that good behaviour is no guarantee of prosperity and success. The concept appears at various points in the play, most notably towards the end (1203-6), where Hecuba remarks that any man who rejoices at the thought that his prosperity will last is a fool; our fortunes jump about like a fickle man, and nobody prospers for ever. In the very year of the play's production Athens sent out to Sicily the expedition which was to end in utter disaster. Nor, despite the sympathy shown by Poseidon and Athena in the Prologue, do the women see the gods as providing any comfort. The Chorus in one of its songs (1060-80) complains that Zeus has betrayed them and does not care.

So far we have considered the way in which Euripides presents the fall of Troy through the eyes of its victims. Even more striking is the fact that these victims are all women. The only male characters to appear, as we have seen, are Talthybius and Menelaus, plus the child Astyanax, who does not have a speaking role. The main characters are all female, Hecuba, Cassandra, Andromache, and Helen. Given the situation this may not be surprising in itself. In ancient warfare when a city is sacked it is only the women who survive to mourn, and lamentation in Greek tradition is in any case the task of women. In Aeschylus' *Persians* the Chorus of male elders certainly laments, the men who were too old to go to war with Xerxes, but Atossa, Xerxes' mother, has a prominent role, and the Chorus frequently refers to the mourning of the Persian women. What is striking about *Trojan Women* is that, more than in any other surviving tragedy, the principal parts, together with that of the Chorus, are all given to women. As so often, our attempt to evaluate the reaction of the fifth-century audience is hampered by uncertainty as to whether it included women. As far as a Greek man was concerned a woman was "the Other", and Euripides is inviting his audience to identify, not only with the foreign Trojans, but more particularly with foreign Trojan women. We may again recall the *Iliad*, in which, as we have seen, the effect of the death of Hector is seen through the eyes of Andromache, and in which Hecuba and Helen join her in the lamentation. More pertinent, however, is a remarkable simile in Book 8 of the *Odyssey*, where Odysseus, on his way home to Ithaca, is being entertained by the Phaeacians on Scheria. His identity has not yet been revealed to his hosts. The bard Demodocus has just told the story of the Wooden Horse and the sack of Troy, and Odysseus is moved to tears. In his weeping he is compared to a woman who falls upon the corpse of her husband who has been killed on the battlefield, fighting in defence of his city. She weeps for him, while the enemy beat her from behind as they try to drag her off into slavery. Odysseus has been the central character in Demodocus' story, and the successful trick of the Wooden Horse has been primarily his achievement. We might therefore expect him to take pride as he is reminded of his part in the capture of Troy. Instead he weeps. He, who was responsible for the sufferings of a sacked city, now identifies himself with the victims of such a sacking, and more particularly with a bereaved woman. Euripides invites his spectators to feel the same compassion for the Trojan women in his play, and it is hard to believe that he does not want that compassion to be extended to the women of Melos. From the point of view of dramatic structure one might expect the play to consist of a continuous and perhaps rather monotonous lament, but in fact the pace is varied, as all four women are treated differently, and we actually see two of them, Hecuba and Helen, engaged in a remarkable conflict, in which the rhetorical structure of their speeches on the philosophical problem of responsibility contrasts effectively with the emotional lamentation that precedes and follows.

It is not unreasonable to describe *Trojan Women* as an anti-war play. But it would be too crude to jump to the conclusion that Euripides is using it to advocate any particular political policy. He, no more than Homer, was a "pacifist" in the modern sense. Like Homer he doubtless saw war as inevitable, and indeed as one of the ways in which a man can obtain glory. But, again like Homer, he shows himself completely aware of the other side of war - the suffering and the loss which are incurred by victor and victim alike. In Aeschylus' *Persians* "the Other" is the barbarian Persians, in Homer and in *Trojan Women* the Trojans, while in the case of the Melians it is Athens' fellow-Greeks who refused to join the Athenian Confederacy. But in every case the audience is encouraged to see itself in "the Other", to recognise the common bond that unites all humanity. *Trojan Women* may have been particularly relevant in 416 B.C., to an audience whose culture was in many respects very different from our own. Yet it is a play that could have been written at any time. It is not surprising that in our own day it is quite often presented on the stage, with the focus shifted by its modern directors and adapters to more recent wars. Like all Greek tragedy it is relevant to the historical and social context in which it was first produced, but at the same time universal in its appeal. Its value transcends the age in which, and the culture for which, it was created, which is what we really mean when we describe a work of literature as a classic.

The *Trojan Women*

Jasper Griffin

In the earlier years of the fifth century it was
the custom for playwrights to compose their
tragedies in coherent trilogies (tetralogies,
counting the satyr play): that is, in a series
linked by a common theme. Our sole
surviving example is the *Oresteia* of
Aeschylus (*Agamemnon*, *Choephoroi*,
Eumenides), dealing with the return of King
Agamemnon from the conquest of Troy, his
murder by his unfaithful wife, the avenging of
that act by his son, and the trial and eventual
acquittal of the son for the killing of his
mother. Both *Suppliant Women* and *Seven
Against Thebes* survive from trilogies of
which, originally, they were only part.

That elaborate and ambitious kind of
composition went out of fashion in the middle
of the century, and the great majority of the
plays both of Sophocles and of Euripides are
single entities, which never formed part of
coherent trilogies; but occasionally
Euripides, at least, returned to something
closer to the older model and composed a
set of plays which presented episodes from
one story, presented in chronological order.
Trojan Women is a striking instance. It was
the last in a set of three plays presented in
415 BC, which were all concerned with
events in the long story of the Trojan War and
the fall of Troy. The other two are lost, but we

know a certain amount about them.

The first was called *Alexandros*. It dealt with the early history of the Trojan prince Paris, also known as Alexandros: at his birth it was predicted that he would be the bane of his country, and so he was as a baby exposed - abandoned in the wild to die. But he did not die. Reared as a shepherd, he proved a handsome and princely youth, who in an athletic contest challenged and defeated his royal brothers. In jealous anger his mother Hecuba plotted with her son Deiphobus to kill this presumptuous upstart; but his true identity was revealed, his life (despite the prophetic warnings of Cassandra) was spared, and he returned in triumph to the city, which he would duly bring to ruin.

The second is set some time later, in the camp of the Greek army besieging Troy. It is called *Palamedes*. He was one of the Greek leaders. Artistic and intellectual, he had invented the art of writing. Odysseus, in this play depicted as an unscrupulous careerist, from jealousy compassed his death. In collusion with King Agamemnon, he faked evidence which appeared to prove him guilty of treasonable dealings with the Trojans; and after a trial Palamedes was put to death. His brother and father were able to devise vengeance for his death, luring a number of Greek ships on to the rocks.

With *Trojan Women* we take another leap forward in time. Troy has now fallen, its men are dead, and we are concerned with the sufferings of the women and children of the captured city. It is not a play rich in events, or in characterisation, or in moral choices. It is in fact a kind of mournful pageant of suffering, its monotonous unfolding of similar inflictions on the poor women itself a depiction of the unending repetition of their griefs. They endure a series of blows at the hands of their conquerors, of whose message Talthybius himself is ashamed and apologises for coming so often with one brutal message after another. The women are divided up, to be separated and taken to different destinations as slaves to one or another of their conquerors.

The princess Cassandra, a consecrated priestess, is to be given as a concubine to the conqueror Agamemnon; she predicts his murder and her own. The princess Polyxena, whom we do not actually see, is sacrificed at the grave of the Greek hero Achilles - killed before the end of the war, he would otherwise have missed out on his share of the captured women. This horrible story is rather played down in this play; the poet had dealt with it at full length in his play *Hecuba*, still extant, another harrowing tragedy of the sufferings of the defeated in war. But we are not spared the death of the child Astyanax, the son of the greatest Trojan hero Hector, whom the victors decide not to allow to grow up and perhaps avenge the defeat of his country. The child is mourned by his mother Andromache and his grandmother Hecuba, the central figure of the play.

And we meet the unfaithful queen Helen, who ran off from her husband with the glamorous Eastern playboy Paris and so caused all the miseries of the war. Recaptured by her husband Menelaus, she is sentenced to death; but she pleads for her life, in a powerful scene in which the aged Hecuba plays the role of prosecutor, and although Menelaus reiterates his determination to kill her, we know that she will in fact be spared and reign serenely back home in Sparta, effortlessly managing her amiable husband. The domesticity of the two is charmingly depicted in the *Odyssey* of Homer, a work familiar to every member of the audience.

In the first play, Paris' life is spared, and he ruins his people. In the second, the innocent Palamedes is judicially murdered; his death will be in a way avenged, but not on the perpetrators, Odysseus and Agamemnon. In the third, we see the misery of the innocent women and children, while the guilty Helen calmly disclaims any responsibility for what has happened. It was all your fault, she tells Hecuba, for having such a son! And it was the fault of Aphrodite, who gave me as a bribe to Paris when he judged the beauty contest among the goddesses! And let's not forget that it was your fault, too, Menelaus: you wretch, you left me alone in the house with him! And despite Hecuba's passionate and rational rebuttal - What you call Aphrodite was your own lustfulness; my son was good looking and stylish, he dazzled a woman in a third world place like Sparta -

Helen gets away with it. Throughout the trilogy, justice is not seen to be done.

What of the conquering Greeks? We see everything that happens in the play in the light of the opening scene, in which the goddess Athena and the sea god Poseidon discuss the past and future. The Greeks have been guilty of a grave sin at the sack of the city; they allowed one of their number to commit sacrilege with impunity, dragging away a woman from Athena's altar. In consequence she has determined, although up to now she has been their ally, to bring disaster on them as they sail home. Poseidon agrees to help, promising storm and wreck: "I shall stir up the Aegean, and the beaches of Myconos, the rocks of Delos, Scyros and Lemnos and Capharea, all shall receive the corpses of many dead men". He closes the scene with the dark moral: "That mortal man is a fool who sacks cities, who ravages their temples and their graves, the sacred possessions of the dead, only to come to grief himself". The Greeks are unaware of this grim future; they do just as they please, with the arrogance of conquerors. But we know that the gods are preparing a very nasty surprise for them, the moment they have torched the city and left for home.

More particularly, we know the fate of the great King Agamemnon himself, who seems to have the world at his feet, and who will not be wrecked on his way home. He will be undone by women, as Troy was. His concubine Cassandra enters, inspired by the prophetic god Apollo. First, she enacts a ghastly parody of a wedding song: Here comes the bride, happy and glorious: congratulate me everyone - I am to be the wife of the King! Talthybius is appalled by this sinister and ill-omened display. Cassandra goes on to foretell the consequences: his adulterous wife is planning his death, and her own; but that means that in the end the Trojans, who seem to have lost, are thoroughly avenged. In fact, they have done better than the victorious Greeks: they lived at home, while their enemies endured the hardships of army and camp; they fought and died nobly for their country, and their name will live in glory - while the Greeks, after years of privation, are to suffer horrible and humiliating deaths, now that the war is over. Talthybius comments drily, "So, the great are no better than the rest of us. The Supreme Commander Agamemnon has picked out this crazy girl. Well, I am a poor man, but I wouldn't want her in my bed..."

The heart of the play is the loving exhibition of the suffering and despair of the women of Troy. Hecuba is on stage throughout. At the opening she is discovered lying prostrate on the ground, grieving for her dead husband Priam, for her dead sons, for her lost kingdom: "I raise a mourning cry, so different from my songs when I led the rhythmic dances of Troy, while Priam leant on his sceptre and watched..." When the captive women elicit from Talthybius the names of the Greek chiefs to whom each is now to be a slave, she learns her own master is to be Odysseus, the wily enemy, the man she hates most in the whole Greek host.

She hears the fate of Polyxena and witnesses the sinister ecstasy of Cassandra, both of them her daughters. The wild scene of Cassandra exulting in her own future death causes Hecuba to lose consciousness and collapse again. She must join her son Hector's widow in lamenting the murder of the grandson who seemed for a moment to be the one hope of Troy; over his broken body she remembers how lovingly he used to talk to her in the old days, while his father Hector was alive, and the city still stood. She argues with Helen and fails to secure her punishment. At the end she tries to throw herself into the fire that is to consume Troy, but she is prevented: she is not her own mistress now but the property of a master.

Hecuba raises the question of the action in all this, or the inaction, of the gods. It was a central function of Attic tragedy to illuminate the ways of heaven to men. The chorus recall that on the fatal night the Trojans were dragging the Horse into Troy, with the intention of offering it to the goddess Athena; it was full of the Greek warriors who would conquer the city. "As for me", sing the women of the chorus, "I was singing and dancing in honour of the goddess Artemis, when a deadly shrieking was heard; children threw their arms round their mothers' skirts, and from their ambush leapt out the armed men, by the will of Pallas Athena..." The event is full of divine agency.

We know from the *Iliad* of Homer that Zeus himself loved Troy. He consented to its ruin only reluctantly, in response to the hatred felt for the city by the goddesses Hera and Athena. Euripides does not miss that effective motif, developing it in a more subjective and pathetic tone. The chorus dwell on the intimate personal links that bound their city to the Olympians. Ganymede, the boy beloved by Zeus, who was carried off to serve as his cup-bearer on Olympus: he is still there, in endless blessedness, "But the city that gave you birth is set ablaze, and the cry of grief goes up all along the shore, some mourning for husbands, some for sons, some for aged mothers; the places where you loved to run and bathe are gone for ever; you keep your bright beauty in the house of Zeus, while the Greek army has destroyed your home land..." Another handsome Trojan, Tithonus, was carried off for his beauty by the goddess of the Dawn, but that, too, means nothing: "The eye of Dawn watched the destruction of our temples... the charm of Troy for the gods is a thing of the past".

Hecuba calls on the gods for justice, or for mercy; her call is in vain. As Cassandra leaves for slavery and death she calls, from a prostrate position on the ground, "O you gods - those are poor allies that I am invoking; and yet there is something in the mere form of invoking the gods". At last, as the Greeks begin to burn the city before they sail away, she cries to them one last time, then says "Why am I calling on the gods? They didn't hear, when they were called on before". The cynicism is striking. The poet goes further, and at moments makes this aged queen of the mythical period, by the sort of sophisticated touch which had a special appeal for Euripides, a surprisingly advanced thinker. Before her big speech denouncing Helen to Menelaus she utters a prayer to unorthodox and high-brow divinities: "O Support of the earth and Enthroned upon it, whoever you are, hard to understand: Zeus, or Natural Necessity, or Human Mind, I pray to you..." We hear echoes of advanced fifth century speculation; poor Menelaus is completely baffled by an utterance so alien to the mythical age and comments, "What did you say? What a new-fangled prayer!"

But mostly her function is the expression of pathos. Old, a widow, a slave, her strong sons gone with her regal splendour, she represents the ultimate example of the power of events to shatter human happiness. She was to be the archetype of tragic misfortune; Hamlet thinks of her at once, when he wants to suggest human misery ("What's he to Hecuba, or she to him, That he should weep?"). When Hector's widow Andromache enters on the wagon which is to take her to captivity, the pair keen in antiphonal lament for their losses and their grief. The poet, who is of course also a musician, arranges their utterances in such a way that in the responding stanza Hecuba sings the passages that were sung by Andromache in the first stanza, and vice versa. Musical virtuosity partly compensates for the studied monotony of the action.

The fall of a city is in a sense the end of the world. We must remind ourselves that among the Greeks each city was an independent state. Its ruin was absolute. In the great war between Athens and her allies, on the one side, and Sparta and her allies, on the other, which lasted from 431 to 404 BC., many cities were besieged, stormed, sacked. The great historian Thucydides tells us that "Never in history were so many cities taken and laid waste" as in that war. The Athenians did their share. Posterity never forgot or forgave the doom of the cities that the Athenians destroyed; especially one whose story was written up at length by Thucydides in his *History*, and which was destroyed in the very year of 415: the little island state of Melos. There the Athenians put the men to the sword and sold the women and children into slavery. Many people have assumed that our play reflects precisely that event.

The chronology is difficult, though: and it seems better to suppose that Euripides is here reflecting back into the mythical period not the single event of Melos, but the fate of many cities which suffered the ultimate disaster in those years. We must also bear in mind that Athens itself was burned to the ground by Xerxes and the Persians in 480, and the temples on the Acropolis were not rebuilt for a generation: the great hill, the sacred centre of the city, was left bare and blackened until the 440's, as a memorial to what the Persians had done, and what Athens had suffered. The resonance of that terrible memory must still have been in the minds of the audience, sitting in the theatre below the Acropolis.

It was not much more than ten years later that the threat uttered by the Melians to Athens in their extremity - Remember that this may happen to you, too - was to come terribly close. When Athens was finally defeated, in 404, the victorious allied cities discussed what should be done to the "tyrant city". The men of Thebes and Corinth were for destroying Athens, as Athens had destroyed Melos, and Torone, and Scione; it might have happened (and we should never have seen the Parthenon); but the Spartans would not have it. And so, by the grace of their greatest enemies, Athens was spared.

An important function of the myth was to serve as a mirror to the present. The martyrdom of Antigone, sentenced to death for opposing an unjust law; the destruction of Pentheus, in the *Bacchae*, brought down by his denial of elements of his own nature; the fate of Troy, the great city that was loved by heaven, and sinned, and was destroyed: these and other myths allowed the audience to see their own world and their own reality more clearly. We recall that Shakespeare set his great tragedies in medieval Scotland,

or Venice, or ancient Rome, or medieval
Denmark, or Britain in the Dark Ages -
anywhere, in fact, but Elizabethan England.

So the doom of Troy, with its inextricable
entanglement of the guilt of Paris and
innocent suffering, served as the mirror in
which to reflect and to make visible and
intelligible the significance of the destruction
of a city in the world of the playwright and of
his audience. Already in the *Iliad* we are
forced to confront the uncomfortable fact that
Paris cannot be punished, and the offence of
stealing a host's wife cannot be undone,
without the ruin of the lives of the women and
children of Troy. We meet Hector's wife, his
child, and his mother. They are attractive
people, and they have done nothing. The
Greek victory, and the righting of a wrong,
cannot be matters of unmixed satisfaction.

That fact, crucial for the whole of Western
sensibility, was developed in Attic tragedy
almost obsessively. Many plays deal with
the possibility or the reality of the destruction
of a city and the suffering of the innocent.
There was no escaping the misery of Hecuba
and Andromache, subjects of so many
tragedies, and the brutal death of Hector's
child. When we remember how many films
we have enjoyed about Bomber Command in
the last war, which never mention the death
of Frau Braun and Frau Schmidt far beneath,
in the destruction (justified, necessary) of
Hamburg or Berlin, we may reflect on the
civilised nature of that insight. We may
reflect, too, if we choose not to stop there,

that appreciation of tragedies, even sensitivity to tragedy to the point of tears, could not, and cannot, be relied on to stop the destruction of cities, or the widowing of women, or the death of children.

Trojan Women:
Sex and the City

Carmel McCallum Barry

Trojan Women is an unsettling play in many ways. Its episodic construction presents us with a succession of scenes each serving to add more misery to the previous ones, so it has no plot in any complex sense, no dénouement of the action such as we see in other tragedies. It is unsettling because it is hard to say what the play is "about", there is such a variety of subject matter and themes to focus on. We could say that it is about war and its aftermath, for it is immediately obvious that we are concerned with the suffering of the victims of war. Euripides makes it clear that the conquerors will suffer too, as the victorious Greeks are guilty of behaviour that will soon bring them misfortune. Such a reversal of fortune fits well with themes of the instability of fortune for humankind and the uncertainty of divine favour, which recur throughout the play. The other important issue that keeps coming up for consideration is that of responsibility; who is to blame for the disasters that have happened and those that are still to come? The most forcible statements from both Trojans and Greeks insist that Helen is the guilty one, responsible for everything.

The diversity of issues explored in the play means that we must look for some larger topic that the play is 'about', one that can include all the rest. I suggest we say that *Trojan Women* is about the annihilation of a city, and for Greeks, who could not consider a full life possible except as members of a city-state, it is an almost apocalyptic vision of the end of a world. The world is a man's world but it is examined through women's suffering; as so often in Euripides' plays problematic issues concerning the city are explored through female characters. The technique is poignantly apt in this play. The women are representative of the sphere of family and personal relationships which underpin any society. When these relationships are expressed in regulated marriage (or 'good Eros' as choruses in drama frequently call it) they are vital to the patriarchal city-state; harmonious and fruitful unions produce new citizens and promote the city's growth and prosperity. In *Trojan Women* it is unhappily clear that marriages or erotic unions in the wider sense are implicated in the city's destruction, no union mentioned in the play has a happy ending. So we have two aspects of social breakdown, state and personal, which constantly interact.

If we consider the play as a tale of the city's destruction the subjects and themes dealt with fit into a tightly constructed pattern; war, suffering, unfortunate marriages, the uncertainty of fortune and the issue of responsibility all form part of the overarching story of the death of Troy. Looking from this point of view we see more clearly that the city has been guilty and is responsible for its own destruction; in the personal sphere it becomes apparent that each disaster mentioned can be linked with a marriage or erotic union. This means of course that the status of the city and of Hecuba as innocent victims is seriously undermined; in Euripides, being a victim is no guarantee of innocence. It also means that we should look more closely at Hecuba, since she is the surviving member of the Trojan royal family, whose destiny can be equated with that of the city. In fact during the course of the play it becomes clear that the guilt of Troy is principally the guilt of its ruling family.

Hecuba was once queen of Troy and now in *Trojan Women* is a symbol of the fallen city, her role is twofold since she is the city but is also one of the women of the title, her griefs stand for theirs. Her identification with Troy is underlined by the language of the play; she lies on the ground as Troy lies in ruins, she falls, trembles and totters as does the city; when the city is set on fire she tries to rush into the flames to become one with it. She exemplifies the pride and wealth of the great city in constantly asserting her once lofty state. As one of the women she will soon, like them, cease to exist as a Trojan, because as well as the destruction of the material remains of the city we are also confronted with the destruction of all its inhabitants, either physically (the male warriors), or by displacement, since the women and children lose their identity when carried off to foreign lands as slaves.

The episodes of the play are linked in the first place by Hecuba's physical presence, but also by the theme of Eros; each successive scene between the individual women and Hecuba presents the subject of unfortunate marriage from a different perspective. Meanwhile the linked choral odes reflect on the ruined life of the ordinary women of Troy and on the problematic unions of the Trojan royal family in the past as well as its culpability on the larger historical canvas.

In the Prologue, Poseidon, hitherto patron of the Trojans, and Athene, supporter of the Greek conquerors, set the scene. Poseidon tells of the defeat of Troy; the streets and holy places run with blood, all the men are dead, King Priam himself has been butchered at the altar of Zeus. The Greeks are now preparing to sail home with their booty which includes the women now waiting to be assigned to their new masters. It is interesting to see that Spartan Helen is considered a Trojan woman and, Poseidon says, is rightly classed among the prisoners. He directs our attention to the aged Hecuba lying on the ground; her husband and sons are dead, one daughter Polyxena has just been sacrificed at the tomb of Achilles and another is a living source of grief. This is Cassandra who is a prophet, intended to remain virgin in the service of the gods, and Apollo has made her into a frenzied prophet because she rejected his advances. She too is one of the prisoners and Agamemnon, leader of the Greeks "will marry her by force", casting aside respect for things divine. Athene enters and shifts focus to the conquerors. She is withdrawing her support from them and wants Poseidon to help in "bringing pleasure to the Trojans and giving the Greeks an unhappy return home". Athene is deserting the Greeks because their leaders did not punish impious offences committed against her in Troy when her temple was violated and the priestess Cassandra forcibly dragged off (raped?). Poseidon agrees to help, for "the man who sacks cities and temples is a fool - he himself perishes later".

The prologue not only gives us background information, it gives us background mood too, a predisposition to feel pity for the suffering women and a willingness to think that the Greeks will get their just deserts. The exchange between the gods is programmatic too, for here at the beginning they demonstrate the interaction between the divine level of activity and the human, both in its collective form as the city and in the individuals who make up the city. Not only has Athena been insulted by the Greeks but Zeus the king of gods has seen the king of Troy cut down at his altar. The uncertainty of divine favour is also made obvious before any human has a chance to complain of it.

After the gods have finished 'setting' the play from a divine perspective, Hecuba does much the same thing from the Trojan point of view. In her opening song she twice refers to her family's former pride and wealth, her former royal status as queen and leader of the women of Troy. She uses imagery connected with ships and sailing to tell herself she must go with the current, not try to sail against the wind. This imagery, which recurs throughout the play, is always ominous.

The chorus of women who enter echo Hecuba's misery and extend the sailing motif to lead into the following scene. The Greeks are ready to sail home, soon the women will learn which chief will be their new master. They lament, not for lost royal status, but for loss of the female routines of ordinary marriage in their native land. No longer will they weave at Trojan looms, carry water from Trojan fountains or see their parents' homes, they mourn for life at home with loved ones, while Hecuba mourns for the pomp of state.

The Greek herald next announces the individual fates of the women of the royal family: Hecuba's daughter Cassandra will have the good fortune to go to the bed of Agamemnon, the other daughter Polyxena, he says enigmatically, will serve the tomb of the dead hero Achilles. Andromache her daughter-in-law, widow of Hector will be taken by the son of Achilles and Hecuba herself will be a slave to Odysseus. The news arouses strong reaction from Hecuba for herself, she cries out against having to serve this treacherous man, a master of double talk, twister of words. The first scene between Hecuba and the individual women follows immediately as flames and smoke are seen and the frenzied Cassandra rushes on waving torches as if for a marriage ceremony. She sings a song of joy for her coming union with Agamemnon, even asks her horrified mother to dance with her. Though Hecuba and the other women are appalled and distressed, the significance of this marriage is clear to Cassandra and to us. It means the death of Agamemnon and the ruin of his family, in fact, the Greeks are less fortunate than the Trojans! Her reasons for this crazy statement make sense within the overall ideology of the play, for they spring from the intimate, family point of view. While besieging Troy, the Greeks could not see their wives and families, they died away from home, denied burial at the hands of their loved ones; the Greek leader actually killed a beloved child in order to go to Troy. The Greek herald perceives the threatening nature of her prophecy, and hurries her off, but Hecuba cannot accept Cassandra's ravings as true, and in a second monody reverts to her own previous proud fortunes. She was born from and married into the ruling family, she produced superior children, but the males are now dead, the girls who were prepared for the best of marriages are now ruined and she, the mother of Hector, now lies as a slave on the floor instead of on a royal bed. It is easy to listen to this story of past grandeur and present misery and feel pity, but we should also listen to the notes of arrogance and excessive pride in the background. Hecuba is Troy in this play, and it is a commonplace in Greek literature that the legendary wealth and pride of Troy led to the city's downfall. The women of the chorus once again take a wider view and in their first ode tell how the blind folly of the Trojans led them to joyous celebrations as they brought the fateful Horse into the city; the recurrent motifs of the play form part of the tale. The Horse was hauled along with ropes like a ship, the celebrations were lit with fiery torches, in the disaster that followed mothers and children were terrified, men slain at altars, and the young women, with no hope of rightful marriage, became a prize of victory for the conquerors, destined to produce children for Greeks, not Trojans. The chorus treat the same themes as Hecuba does but reflect on the fate of the city as a whole rather than on that of the royal family as the city.

Their reflections lead naturally into the next episode and the entry of Andromache, carrying her child, the son of Hector; she is being taken off to serve the bed of Achilles' son. She brings Hecuba news of fresh misery, that Polyxena has been sacrificed as a gift to the dead Achilles. This princess of Troy, prepared by her mother for a noble marriage has become the bride of death, as will Cassandra. Andromache, however feels that Polyxena is fortunate to be dead, and speaks of her own fortunes in marriage. She was a model wife to Hector, behaved properly in every way, her reward now is that her high reputation has made her desirable to the son of the man who killed her husband. "I shall be a slave in the house of murderers". Her dilemma is serious, if she goes willingly to the bed of her new master she will be a traitor to Hector's memory; on the other hand if she does not go willingly she will be hated by her master. It is equally serious for the issues of the play, as whatever she does will involve betrayal of one of the marriages. She concludes that death is preferable to having to make the choice. Hecuba's response is startling, she begins thoughts of sailing on a sea of troubles, then advises Andromache to stop mourning Hector and honour her new husband, advice which seems callous and at variance with her character as established so far. But it is consistent with what she has already said in sea of troubles' vein and it echoes her previous resolve to go with the currents, because the course she recommends is a way for Troy to survive. If Andromache can co-exist with Achilles' son she can bring up her own and Hector's child in safety. The child's name, Astyanax means 'lord of the city', like Hecabe he is a symbol of Troy, so his survival can mean survival of the city.

However as we might expect, such hopes are doomed, and immediately the herald announces that the Greeks have no intention of allowing a male of the Trojan royal family to survive; Astyanax is to be killed by being thrown from the walls of Troy. Andromache's marriage is revealed after all as a tragic one, "a bed and marriage unfortunate" (745), "a fine marriage I am going to, when I have lost my child" (778-9) she says. The chorus pick up the thought, Troy has lost all her children for the sake of one woman (Helen) and her hateful marriage; once more the city and its continued life are linked to the quality of marriage.

In this ode the chorus goes back in time and probes earlier episodes in Trojan history. It is often said that the content intensifies the sympathy we feel for Troy, but I think not. On the contrary, it demonstrates once again that Troy and its royal family are in no small way deserving of blame, and that in the past also unfortunate erotic unions played a part in disaster for Troy. In the ode's complex mythological frame of reference events actually narrated and others that are inferred reveal Troy and its royal family as doomed and culpable in the previous generation. The story according to the chorus is that Heracles rescued the daughter of King Laomedon (Priam's father) from a sea monster, as a reward Laomedon had promised to give the hero mares of a breed given to him by Zeus. But Laomedon cheated the hero of his reward so Heracles led an expedition against Troy and sacked the city. There is no judgement made but a parallel can be drawn with the present situation. What is not mentioned in the ode, but all would know, is that Laomedon made a habit of faithlessness. He had even reneged on his agreement with the gods Apollo and Poseidon, by refusing to pay them for helping to build the walls of Troy. The chorus continues with a reference to Laomedon's son Ganymede who was loved by Zeus and taken to be his cupbearer on Olympus. It appears that the Trojans expected some special treatment from the gods because of Ganymede's favour on Olympus, but in vain, "you beside the throne of Zeus keep your face beautiful in its calm". This love affair is the only non problematic union mentioned in the play, the reason perhaps is simply that both Zeus and Ganymede are totally detached, uninvolved in Trojan woes. One other amorous relationship linking Troy and its royal family with the gods is alluded to briefly, but significantly in a section beginning with an invocation to Eros, Eros who came from the gods and made Troy great. The love referred to is that of the goddess of the Dawn for Tithonus, another son of Laomedon, whom she persuaded Zeus to make immortal. The union brought no benefit to Troy and only flawed happiness for Tithonus, for according to other versions of the myth, he was not given immortal youth, and the goddess grew tired of her ageing lover. The last line of this ode sums up everything for Troy, "the charms of love with the gods are gone".

This choral ode encapsulates present as well as past problems of Troy. These problems clearly derive from the royal family which was loved by the gods in the past, but treachery on the part of humans led to the destruction of the city itself. This fatal combination is strongly marked as the real dynamic of the play by its reappearance in the following dramatic episode. The same associations of Trojans, gods, Eros/marriage and betrayal form the subject of debate when Helen is brought to face Hecuba and Menelaus, the husband she abandoned to go with Paris to Troy. Menelaus insists that he came to Troy, not so much to get back Helen, but for revenge on Paris who had betrayed the code of hospitality when he was a guest of Menelaus in Sparta. The Trojans now have paid the price for this treachery; as for Helen, he will take her by ship back to Greece and there put her to death. Hecuba at this point moves out of the passive role that she has played so far, accepting the blows of misfortune. She begs Menelaus to kill Helen here in Troy, and persuades him to allow a debate in which Hecuba herself will be prosecutor. Helen speaks first, her defence like the preceding choral ode brings together the important themes of marriage and responsibility for the war; however she does not confine herself to accusing Trojans for what has happened. She blames Hecuba for giving birth to Paris, Priam for not killing him once he was born; she goes on to blame the three goddesses who made Paris the judge of their beauty, especially Aphrodite who caused her to fall in love with Paris. Helen adds to the list of usual suspects; she further accuses Menelaus for leaving home while Paris was there, the Trojans who stopped her escaping once Paris was dead and Deiphobus who then forced her to become his wife. It is a common criticism of Helen in this scene that she appears foolish and shallow, her arguments as specious and ridiculous. Maybe so, but her rhetoric is no less slippery than that of Hecuba when she comes to speak and it is in keeping with the information we are given in the rest of the play to consider everyone as in some way guilty of the total dissolution of the world of the city which the fall of Troy represents. Hecuba's response is disappointing, she loses some of her tragic dignity in her attack upon Helen, and her argumentation is no more convincing. Her speech also shows a confusion of values in her eagerness to condemn Helen; she says that Helen should have committed suicide when compelled to remain in Troy after Paris's death "this is what a noble woman would have done", and yet she advised Andromache not to wish for death but accommodate herself to her new husband! Finally, in the name of the children of the Greeks (!) who have died, she pleads for Helen's execution. This episode of debate once more links Greeks and Trojans in the same pattern of guilt, indeed it is difficult to find sympathy for any of the speakers in the debate. Problems have arisen from the marriage of Helen and Menelaus but also from that of Hecuba and Priam who had been warned when she was pregnant with Paris that if allowed to survive he would destroy Troy. In a way the Greeks are only the mechanism of Troy's destruction which had been made inevitable by the flawed relations between Trojans and gods.

The last choral ode recapitulates the fall of Troy and its implications. The gods seem not to care about honours paid to them by Trojans in the past, for now husbands lie unburied while wives and children are taken off into slavery and Helen still lives. Our sympathy is roused for Hecuba once more as she attends to the burial of Astyanax, although even in this she still clings to fabled Trojan pride. She mourns for the child who never had a share of the glory of Troy, a fine marriage, power and rule equal to that of the gods.

After Troy's future is wiped out with Astyanax, all that remains is to burn the city to the ground and remove the women to their new marriages. Hecuba attempts to rush into the flames, demonstrating as at the beginning of the play, her oneness with the city. The final dissolution describes Troy and Hecuba identically, collapsing to the ground.

Trojan Women may be episodic in construction but it is not unstructured. Every scene and choral ode is integrated and orchestrated towards this ending where we witness the complete dissolution of the city, and everything that it consists of: its wealth, walls, laws, religious rituals and family kinship groups. The causes of the disaster lie in Troy itself. Trojans have broken faith with the gods and with human conventions and relationships which the gods are thought to oversee. These include the sanctity of oaths, kingship, hospitality and family integrity. We are accustomed to see in Greek drama a view of marriage as the foundation of a prosperous city (*Eumenides* gives this notion its fullest expression). The other possibility presented here is that it can also be the ruin of the city. What makes the play satisfying as tragedy and appealing today is not just its harrowing look at the victims of war, but its moral ambiguity. Our sympathies are engaged for the suffering victims and we feel outrage at the brutality of the conquerors, but sadly the victims are not without blame.

Although we interpret the play for ourselves in the light of modern experience and behavioural standards we should not lose sight of its significance in its own time. This grim picture of a society destroyed by war with further disasters in prospect for the conquerors was presented by Euripides in 415 BC, when Athens had been at war for over fifteen years, but was still ten years away from final defeat. It is possible to read the play as directly related to contemporary situations, as a cautionary tale for Athenians, possibly a warning against arrogant, impious behaviour. However such an interpretation is optimistic, it implies that things can get better, and there is no justification for this in *Trojan Women*. We see that the community or state is sick and that the sickness spreads down from the top, affecting even those parts that seem to function properly, the families of ordinary Trojan men and women. The theme of the disintegration of the city or public community, together with the related theme of the breakdown of marriage relationships continued to occupy Euripides, as we can see from the two plays produced after his death when Athens was close to defeat.

In *Iphigeneia at Aulis* the demands of state destroy a family. Compelled by the people who are eager to go to war, Agamemnon decides to sacrifice his daughter, thus attacking his own family and giving Clytemnestra reasons to hate him. As in *Trojan Women*, all marriages mentioned in *Iphigeneia* are problematic and the depiction of the heroic leaders is anything but reassuring. However in *Bacchae*, probably produced in the same year (404 BC), we find the most complete and appalling picture of the disintegration of state and family alike. The disasters which befall the city of Thebes are also causally linked with men's behaviour towards the gods, and Dionysus as a character in the play coolly plans the details of destruction. *Trojan Women* therefore, like the words of Poseidon in the Prologue warns us of worse things to come.

The Cassandra Scene

Richard Rutherford

I shall discuss a single scene in the play, and try to define its dramatic and its distinctively Euripidean qualities. The *Trojan Women* begins with the majestic yet chilling encounter between Poseidon and Athena, in which they make a compact to send storms to scatter and reduce the returning Greek fleet. Thereafter we move to the human level of action, and witness the miserable laments of Hecuba and the women of Troy. Thus far the play has been static, but the next sequence strikes a much more rapid and agitated note.

The scene I shall consider is the one in which the prophetess Cassandra enters in a state of wild excitement, exulting in her "marriage" to Agamemnon, leader of the conquering army. The Greek herald Talthybius, conversing with Queen Hecuba, observes a burst of torch-flame from within the women's shelter. He reacts with alarm, fearing the women indoors have decided to burn themselves to death. Hecuba reassures him: "There is no fire. My daughter, Cassandra, in her madness is rushing out here in a frenzy." A moment later Cassandra enters bearing torches, as though celebrating her own wedding. Her entrance song includes appeals to the god Hymenaeus, who presides over marriage: in this first section she sings, in wild and emotional metres. In the second part of the scene she calms down somewhat, enough to revert to normal spoken verse, and speaks more lucidly to her mother. But her words are still allusive and hard for the others to comprehend, as she foretells the misfortunes of the Greeks on their journey home, the interminable wanderings of Odysseus, and the humiliating end that awaits the triumphant Agamemnon. It is a traditional feature of the legend that Cassandra's prophecies should not be believed, and neither the sympathetic Hecuba nor the contemptuous Talthybius recognise the truly ominous significance of her warnings. At the end of the scene she is led away to the ships, bidding farewell to her mother and her homeland, and anticipating her own death at Mycenae. From entrance to exit she has dominated the stage for just over 150 lines; but she does not reappear in the play, and we are probably meant to suppose that her mother never sees her again. Cassandra, like other women in this play, is a victim of war and thus arouses our pity, but what other functions does this striking episode perform in the play?

The first point to make is one which looks back beyond Euripides to his great predecessor Aeschylus. The scene is in part a tribute to, and imitation of, the Cassandra scene in Aeschylus' *Agamemnon*, over four decades earlier. In that play, Agamemnon brings Cassandra home as a concubine, but she is a silent witness while Clytemnestra welcomes her husband home with hypocritical extravagance. Only after he has been lured inside does she break silence, and there too her utterances are first delivered in impassioned lyrics; only gradually does she shake off the burden of divine inspiration and speak more straightforwardly to the chorus. There too she prophesies Agamemnon's death and her own; there too she renounces the trappings of Apollo; there too her predictions only confuse her audience, who do not understand or credit her words. What is different in Euripides is the tone of Cassandra's response to the situation: whereas in Aeschylus her mood is bitter yet resigned, in the new scene she is at first ecstatic in celebration of her "wedding", then argues at length for the paradoxical conclusion that the Trojans are happier than the Greeks. The rhetorical ingenuity is typical of Euripides, and redolent of the age of the sophists: in the same way, Helen later argues that her abandonment of Menelaus was actually beneficial to Greece! Eccentric argumentation of this kind is not found in Aeschylus, and contributes to the more cerebral character of Euripidean tragedy. Emotional moments are handled in a complex though still moving way.

A second important point is that although this scene is the only one in which we, the modern audience, see Cassandra, we know that she appeared earlier in the trilogy. Euripides did not normally go in for connected trilogies, preferring to compose self-contained plays, but the Trojan trilogy of 415 was an exception. The first play, the *Alexandros*, concerned Paris's upbringing after being exposed as a child, and his reinstatement as a prince of Troy. The second, *Palamedes*, dealt with an episode on the Greek side during the course of the war. Neither survives, but we know a certain amount about them from indirect evidence. In particular, it seems clear that Cassandra spoke the prologue of the first play, and that she described the danger that threatened Troy if Paris (Alexandros) was allowed to live: he would prove to be "the ruin of Troy and the destruction of Pergamum". However the plot of that play worked in detail, it is obvious that Cassandra's warnings were given in vain: Paris survived, was recognised and welcomed back as a favoured son, and proceeded to carry off Helen and bring retribution on Troy. Now, in the third play, Cassandra reappears and prophesies again. This time, the burden of her prediction is that the Greeks will pay dearly for their victory, and she presents this as cause for celebration and rejoicing among the Trojans. Her record so far makes the audience confident that this prophecy is true (it is confirmed not only by the tradition but also by the dialogue of Poseidon and Athena in this play); but this is cold comfort for the Trojans even if they did believe her - which they do not. The futility of Cassandra's prophetic gift is highlighted in both the *Alexandros* and the *Trojan Women*.

Thirdly, the dramatic technique of the scene

needs some attention, and especially the formal aspects of song, speech, and genre. The first part of the sequence, from Cassandra's entry at a run (307), involves wild and agitated song from the inspired maiden, who calls on Hymenaeus, Hecate and Apollo in a frenzied version of a marriage-song. At 342 the poet reverts to spoken verse (iambic trimeters, the normal metre for regular speech): the chorus-leader urges Hecuba to restrain Cassandra and prevent her from running off to the Greek camp, and Hecuba tries to recall her daughter to sanity. Cassandra's response is a long speech (353-405) in which she encourages her mother to rejoice, alludes to Agamemnon's death, and presents her arguments for the misery of the Greeks (they undertook a war for a bad woman, many of them died here, meanwhile their wives died childless back at home), and for the happiness of the Trojans (they died gloriously, fighting for their country; they were able to go home after the day's fighting, to their families; Hector was fortunate, because he, like the rest of the Trojans, gained undying fame from the war - which they could never have had if not for Paris's crime!).

The chorus replies with a couplet of discontented bewilderment, referring to the obscurity of her words. Talthybius the herald is sterner: if she were not out of her mind, she would be punished for this sort of talk; and Agamemnon is a fool to fancy such a crazed woman (408ff.). This turns

Cassandra's attention toward him: in another long speech she first denounces the sycophantic race of heralds, then reverts to foretelling misfortunes for the Greeks, including a catalogue of trials which will face Odysseus (424-443). Finally, her speech shifts from iambic trimeters to trochaic tetrameters, a longer line and a metre that Euripides seems regularly to use for scenes of fast movement, agitation or excitement; this is a signal that the emotional tempo and the frenzy of her inspiration - or her madness - are again on the increase. In this final section she reverts to the language of marriage, but with blacker and more macabre references to her own death and that of her "bridegroom": "let me marry my bridegroom in the house of Hades" (445); "they will toss me out as a naked corpse, and the ravines will give me to wild beasts as their food, near my groom's grave..." (448-9). In this section Cassandra's impatience is growing: bizarrely, she is eager to go aboard the ship which is to convey her into exile and slavery, unlike the rest of the women who dread the prospect of enslavement in foreign lands. She sees herself as an instrument of vengeance, a Fury; in conclusion, she declares that her forthcoming death will be an occasion for triumph: "I will come victorious to the dead, after sacking the halls of the Atridae, by whom we were ruined." (460-1)

This description makes clear that the scene requires a virtuoso performance from the actor who plays Cassandra. The character swings between ecstatic inspiration and vigorous rationality; the mode of presentation alters in relation to this shift, from agitated singing to more measured but eloquent argument and up the scale again to emotional prophetic assertion. This kind of modulation between song and speech can be paralleled elsewhere in Greek tragedy: it figures in the scene in the *Agamemnon* which Euripides is imitating, and in other scenes involving passionate female characters in Euripides (the death of Alcestis in the play of that name; the delirium of Phaedra in *Hippolytus*, where the heroine eventually recovers her self-control and speaks more rationally). Here there is a generic aspect too: the earlier part of the scene is a kind of parody of a wedding song, as is shown not only by the invocations of Hymenaeus but by phrases such as "blessed is the bridegroom" (311). Where a wedding-celebration should be a communal event, Cassandra here celebrates on her own, without support or justification: Agamemnon is not present, nor is the relationship which he contemplates with her one of marriage. Later indeed she speaks of the marriage as one which will be celebrated in Hades (see above). This kind of distortion of ritual, whereby something familiar and positive is transformed into a parodic or horrific form, is an extremely powerful and significant element in Greek tragedy: another example is the perversion of sacrificial ritual, as in the human sacrifice of figures such as Iphigenia and Polyxena.

Just as the wedding-song is distorted and negated, so also is the formal rhetoric which Cassandra deploys in the second part of the scene. Rhetoric, as practised in the assembly and lawcourts of Euripides' time, is normally regarded as the art of persuasion. At least ideally, it utilises reasoned arguments from evidence to reach generally acceptable conclusions with practical consequences. Here we see a kind of parodic rhetoric. First, the case which Cassandra is arguing is paradoxical, unbelievable, unacceptable to any of those present: neither the victorious Greeks nor the vanquished Trojans are going to agree that the Trojans are happier or better off than the Greeks. Second, in a normal rhetorical scenario it may be unlikely that an opponent will be convinced, but it is not impossible. In Cassandra's case, however, it is a fundamental feature of her mythic character, already familiar to Aeschylus' audience and certainly to Euripides', that her prophecies are not believed; so there is no chance of her convincing her audience of the truth of what she predicts. Thirdly, even if she did convince them, this can have no practical consequences. If Hecuba were, impossibly, to say "yes, you are right; the Trojans haven't had such a bad deal after all", it would make no difference to the sufferings in store. When characters in tragedy know the truth about the future, it rarely brings them much comfort: Oedipus' inadequate foresight is a case in point. Fourth, although Cassandra's vision of the future is obviously true, for we know Agamemnon will die and the other

Greeks will indeed suffer, her attitude to the whole situation remains peculiar, her reasoning skewed. Is this divine insight also a kind of delusion or insanity which leads her to see things in a false light? When Talthybius dismisses her as a madwoman, he clearly does not look deep enough into what she says, but he is not altogether wrong either. The scene certainly leaves us unsure how to assess Cassandra, how far we should endorse her conviction that she will be the instrument of retribution for her people. Is this more than a grandiloquent piece of self-deception?

In both the sung and the spoken sections, then, we see a clearly deliberate distortion of generic conventions, which enhances our sense of the world of the play as a world in which all that is normal, comfortable or familiar to the women of Troy has been destroyed. Other parts of the play reinforce this perception: for example, the choral ode which follows the episode that includes the Cassandra scene, in which the women recall the ritual celebrations, song, music and public worship which followed the apparent departure of the Greek forces - celebrations which were then interrupted by the "bloodthirsty shout" of warriors emerging from the horse.

It remains to say something about the place of the Cassandra scene in the structure of the *Trojan Women* as a whole. Although, as we have seen, there are connections on the level of plot with the rest of the trilogy

(Cassandra prophesied evil to come in the first play, and now does so again), this still remains a strikingly self-contained and independent episode. Hecuba has barely reacted to the departure of Cassandra before further misfortunes ensue. Even in the speech she makes immediately after her daughter's exit, Cassandra's sorrows are only one topic among many: she is paired with Polyxena, and Hecuba as queen and royal mother sees herself as burdened by the catastrophe of all Troy. Some of the later scenes are dominated by Andromache and the fate of her son Astyanax, and by the confrontation of Hecuba with Helen; others are given up to lamentation and mourning for what is lost. This is not a tragedy which fits well with Aristotle's requirements that a drama should present an action, and that plot should follow a necessary or probable sequence. There is no obvious reason arising from the plot for the Cassandra scene to come where it does, as opposed to later in the play, although there may be dramatic motivations for placing it early. The scene, that is, affects the audience emotionally, but has no consequences for the succeeding events of the play. Rather, the *Trojan Women* is made up of virtually self-contained episodes strung together, united by the continuous presence of the queen and the chorus, individual and collective victims of the Greek victory.

To point this out is not to criticise the playwright. Aristotle also remarked, with rather patronising praise, that "whatever other defects of organisation Euripides may have, he is the most intensely tragic of all the poets" - that is, the most skilled at arousing pity and fear, the quintessentially tragic emotions. Indeed, rather than assume that, living before Aristotle, he was not well-instructed enough in what a tragic plot ought to look like, it is better to allow that the dramatists could innovate, in structuring their plays as in the detail of the myths they used. If the *Trojan Women* lacks the "necessary or probable sequence" of action, if it does not possess the forward impetus of the *Oedipus* or the *Medea*, that in itself may be expressive. Action by Hecuba, by Cassandra, by Andromache, by any of the women of Troy, is impossible. They are the victims; the trophies of war are passive. This is not a play about heroic action or initiative or self-sacrifice. At most it is a play of suffering, which is indeed intense and prolonged but which it would be strange to call heroic. As in other places (for instance, the *Heracles*), Euripides uses structure to convey meaning - to express through a series of exceptionally bleak and uncompromising episodes the unalloyed horror that follows on total defeat in war. Whether we focus on Cassandra's delusion or Hecuba's despair, the *Trojan Women* is a tragedy as dark as any in the Greek canon.

Because the continuum of myth extends beyond the fate of a single individual or family or even a single city, every Greek tragedy ends with something else still in store. In some tragedies closure is imposed more firmly than in others, but in many the events still in store are of great importance in shaping our attitude to the whole play. In Euripides' *Medea*, the Athenian audience would have been aware that Medea would not only find refuge in Athens (as foreseen with dismay by the chorus of that play) but would gain an ascendancy over gullible King Aegeus and eventually threaten the life of the Athenians' favourite hero Theseus. At the conclusion of Sophocles' *Oedipus at Colonos*, Antigone departs for Thebes, determined to bury her brother Polynices; the whole plot of the *Antigone* is foreshadowed, making very clear that the passing of old Oedipus does not bring the action to a final or satisfying close.

What of the aftermath of the *Trojan Women*? It is obvious that Euripides intends to keep the subsequent events very much in our minds: the dialogue between Athena and Poseidon predicts the dispersal of the Greek fleet; the Trojan women anxiously wonder who their masters will be, and where they will each be taken; the prophecies of Cassandra foretell the fate of Agamemnon and Odysseus, as well as the transformation of her mother into animal form; the Helen-scene anticipates the renewed infatuation of Menelaus with his guileful and beguiling wife. In a way, then, the Trojan sufferings are balanced by the future sufferings of the Greeks; but it is obvious that this does not cancel out the present agonies of those who have lost their city, or of Andromache who has lost her husband and within the play has to lose her son to a particularly brutal and barbaric death. According to Cassandra, she is the victor, and the Trojans are happier than the Greeks. This conviction, though it may be divinely inspired, is denied by any human audience of the play. Euripides seems to have included the Cassandra scene in part to show how futile such calculations of future compensation must be when the present suffering is real and undeniable and immediate. "Look to the end" is traditional Greek wisdom, and comes naturally to one who is detached, an onlooker or adviser (like Solon in Herodotus). When it comes from one who is herself involved in calamity, it can only bring consolation because she is mad.

Discussion of the conclusions of plays and tales provides a suitable point of closure, and it is time that this already over-long essay reached its end.

Trojan Women -
An Ancient Music Drama?

David Raeburn

Trojan Women is a tragedy about the fall of a great city and the suffering which war inflicts, particularly on innocent women and children. When it has been revived in modern times, it has been natural to treat it as a critical denunciation of war. Moreover, the historical context of the first performance suggests that Euripides may have wanted to make that kind of statement. However, when we look at the form and experience the sound of the original Greek text, we may discover that it bears interesting similarities to Italian grand opera or Wagnerian music drama which uses music to express human emotions or to describe calamitous happenings. This discovery need not necessarily affect the way in which we interpret the play's meaning, but it may affect the balance between thought and feeling in our response to the drama.

Before we examine the detail of *Trojan Women* in this light, it may be useful to say something about the forms and musical patterns to be found in all Greek tragedies, as some readers may not be familiar with them.

To start with, tragedies in ancient Athens were composed in verse and designed to be performed by a Chorus and three solo actors who divided all the different roles between them. (Non-speaking parts like guards and handmaidens etc. were "extra" to the main performing team.) The poets had to structure the story they were telling in distinct "movements" for soloists and Chorus, but to do so in such a way that the sequence flowed logically and naturally within the shape of the drama as a whole.

As a general rule the movements for the actors were *spoken*, while those for the Chorus were *sung* to the musical accompaniment of an instrument called the *aulos* or reed-pipe. The choral songs also involved formally choreographed movement, but we can only speculate on what this might have been like. It is commonly said that the original music to tragedy is also lost, but that is not entirely true. The *words* of the plays we have inherited contain a great deal of music in themselves. This is to be seen first in the natural rise and fall of the voice as determined by the tonic (pitch) accentuation of ancient Greek; declaimed poetry thus contains a kind of melody of its own. Secondly, with a little technical knowledge, we can easily respond to the *rhythms* (metres) which the poets used for the different utterances of soloists and Chorus. Remember too that these plays were performed in large open-air theatres where vocal projection would have been all-important throughout.

More needs to be said about metres and the

distinction between speech and singing. The words to be declaimed by the solo actors in their "episodes" were composed in an *iambic* verse-form, not altogether unlike Shakespearian verse. The choral songs, by contrast, were constructed in much more complicated and varied rhythmical patterns. The metres of these are generally referred to as *lyric* and are fascinating to study and respond to as a kind of music in their own right. When these are employed, they tend to lift the drama on to a higher level of emotional intensity. We thus have two primary "modes of utterance", associated respectively with soloists and Chorus. We may note, though, that we sometimes find brief interventions in iambic mode from a representative or "leader" of the Chorus. More excitingly, at moments of special poignancy, the actors themselves move from iambic to lyric mode and burst into song, either on their own or in dialogue with the Chorus. These moments are ones to be specially looked for and particularly enjoyed.

Between these two main modes, there is a kind of half-way house, used by soloists and Chorus alike, in an anapaestic rhythm, of the character: di-di-dúm di-di-dúm di-di-dúm di-di-dúm. Delivery in this metre, as a rule, probably approximated more closely to the spoken mode; but it does sometimes seem to have been raised to lyric (sung) mode, with a slowing-down of the rhythm achieved by substituting one long syllable for two shorts. Anapaests are used in a variety of contexts, including short transitional passages for (probably) the Chorus leader designed to cover a new entrance. The metre features prominently in *Trojan Women*.

One further point needs to be made about the form of the iambic movements delivered by the soloists. These mostly consist *either* of long elaborately structured speeches (telling a story, arguing a point or expressing a character's emotions) *or* of fast-moving single line dialogue between two characters, called *stichomythia*, which the Greek dramatists found an excellent medium for the expression of conflict. Occasionally the actors respond to each other in pairs of lines (*distichomythia*) and this results in a more staid exchange. At moments of extreme tension, half-lines are briefly resorted to, with very exciting effect.

Newcomers to Greek tragedy will thus appreciate that these old poetic plays are composed in a highly formalized way, in a style quite alien to that of modern realistic drama. Formally speaking, they can be compared with 18th century opera or oratorio; and it makes sense to think of the long speeches as "arias" and the *stichomythia* as a kind of "recitative". In *Trojan Women* we shall see that some of the long speeches are actually referred to in the language of music rather than of ordinary speech.

Let us now look at *Trojan Women* itself as a musico-dramatic sequence. I have divided the play into scenes to indicate the main structure but emphasize that it should be seen as a seamless robe.

Scene 1 (lines 1-97) Prologue

The opening scene, though assigned to two gods, is not pitched at too intense a level. Euripides starts in his usual manner with a monologue by the sea god, Poseidon, who has been friendly to Troy. He explains the setting and the situation: Troy is now smouldering after its sack by the Greeks, whose leaders are shortly to sail home with the captive Trojan women as their slaves and concubines. He mentions Helen and Cassandra, who will appear later in the play, and also introduces Hecuba, the murdered Priam's queen, who is already onstage "lying in front of the entrance". Poseidon's farewell to Troy at the end of his long speech returns to the key motif of a great city's fall.

Enter the second divinity, Athena, who has previously supported the Greeks but has now turned against them. She and Poseidon warily make common cause in a passage of *distichomythia*, yielding to faster flowing *stichomythia*, which in this context suggests that the two gods are now getting on really well. Then, in a speech of ten lines, Athena asks Poseidon, with Zeus' help, to raise a storm which will destroy the Greek fleet on its return home; and in a balancing speech of almost the same length Poseidon agrees. He concludes with the grim reflection that sacking of cities with their shrines and sacred possessions is as destructive to the conqueror as to the conquered. That is the background against which Euripides invites us to view and sympathize with the suffering and maltreatment of the Trojan women, with whom the play from now on is concerned.

Scene 2 (lines 98-229), including entrance of Chorus.

After the fairly quiet but sinister prologue, the "music" begins. The prostrate Queen Hecuba raises her head and in spoken anapaests slowly starts to lament her humiliation and all that she has lost. Her dirge doubtless swells to a chant as she physically rocks her body in her grief. She has probably risen to her feet when she launches into lyric anapaests, that is proper song, to describe the initial voyage of the Greek ships to Troy to the accompaniment of *auloi* (reed pipes) and *syringes* (panpipes). This may well suggest that Hecuba herself is singing to some kind of musical accompaniment as her lament rises to a higher level of poignancy. At the climax she calls on the Trojan women to join in her cries of *aiai* and contrasts the *song* she will be leading with the singing and dancing she once led in honour of Troy's gods when Priam was alive.

Euripides brings on his Chorus of Trojan women rather unusually, in two half-sections. The first group joins Hecuba in an anapaestic dialogue as they express their fears for their future fate. Then the second semi-chorus enters and their exchange with the queen precisely replicates the pattern of the first one, both metrically and in the division of the verse. This illustrates the typical choral structure of *strophe* and *antistrophe*, a kind of symmetry which is essential to the musical patterning of Greek tragedy. It also looks as if each semi-chorus's anapaests are of the normal type, while Hecuba sticks to the slower lyric kind. This would produce a subtle and interesting musical contrast, particularly if Hecuba's lines were accompanied by an instrument, where the half-choruses were not.

The full Chorus is now assembled and can sing for the first time on their own in unison, to envisage the different cities on the mainland of Greece or in its colonies to which they might be taken as captives. Their anapaests are now of the full lyric type, to suggest that their feelings are rising to Hecuba's level, though their song seems gradually to become more tranquil as they consider the more attractive places in which they might be called to live.

Scene 3 (lines 230-460) Talthybius and Cassandra

The pace quickens as the Chorus leader, returning briefly to normal spoken anapaests, announces the hasty arrival of Talthybius, the Greek herald, who has come to announce the allotment of the Trojan women to their new masters. Hecuba's daughter, Cassandra, has to go to Agamemnon; while Achilles' son,

Neoptolemus, has won Andromache, the wife of Hecuba's son, Hector. One other daughter, Polyxena, is also mentioned and said mysteriously to have been assigned to Achilles' tomb - she has, in fact, been sacrificed on it. Hecuba herself belongs to Odysseus. This information is relayed in an unusual exchange with Talthybius speaking in single iambic lines, while Hecuba questions and reacts in a variety of wild, sometimes irregular, lyric metres expressive of her profound agitation. Once again, Euripides seems to have deliberately combined the spoken and sung modes to achieve a special kind of musical effect. The climax of this is Hecuba's horrified reaction to the prospect of the villainous Odysseus as her lord, and her savage denunciation of him is composed in an extended passage of violently contrasting rhythmical phrases.

The tension continues as Talthybius, still in iambic, orders Cassandra to be brought from the stage-building (representing the women's quarters) to be taken to Agamemnon. But it looks as if the house is on fire! Could this be an attempt to mass-suicide among the captives?

No, it is Cassandra, the mad prophetess, who enters bearing torches and rushes round the acting area in a strange dance purporting to be an ecstatic celebration of her impending marriage to Agamemnon. In the virgin seer, dedicated to Apollo, this is bizarre. Frenetic metres can be heard again in Cassandra's song, as she invokes Apollo and Hymen, the god of marriage, and tries to get her poor old mother dancing around in a circle with her - a sensational 'number'!

After so much excitement we need to settle back into normal iambic mode. In a shortish speech Hecuba tries to calm her frenzied daughter down and manages to relieve her of her two torches. Cassandra responds in a speech of over fifty lines, in which she justifies her strange joy in more rational terms. The union with Agamemnon will lead to his death and the destruction of his house - besides her own death. She then embarks on an elaborate demonstration that the war has really brought more suffering to the Greeks than it has to the Trojans. The rhetorical tone of this speech is in marked contrast to Cassandra's wild lyrics, but it can still be described as a kind of aria, as may be suggested by the song-language used by the Chorus leader immediately afterwards (407) to describe Cassandra's prophecies.

Talthybius' reply to Cassandra is briefer. He does not think much of Agamemnon for wanting this mad woman as his partner in bed! He orders her to follow him to the ships while Hecuba waits for Odysseus. But Cassandra has one more long speech to go before she makes her exit. In twenty iambic lines she castigates the herald for his pretensions and prophesies that Odysseus will undergo an appalling series of dangers on his homeward journey, returning only to find a mass of troubles in store. The metre then changes to long trochaic lines of the pattern: 'Leáve Odýsseus tó his wánderings, lét me fínd my mán in Deáth!' The pace quickens excitingly as Cassandra's prophetic mood returns. She tears away the fillets which signified her dedication to Apollo and rushes off in exultant triumph at the thought of the destruction she will bring on Agamemnon's house.

At the end of this extraordinary scene, Hecuba collapses on the ground. Some attendants try to lift her up, but she asks to be left alone. It is now her turn for a long aria (45 lines) which she describes (472) as a kind of swan-song. She contrasts the blessings she once enjoyed with the bereavements she has suffered and the life of slavery ahead. At the end she asks to be led back to her pallet-bed in front of the house and lies down there once more. The mood of Cassandra's triumph has yielded to deep gloom at the fickleness of human fortune.

Choral Song 1 (lines 511-67)

Now follows the first of three magnificent choral odes, which should not be seen as mere interludes but rather as three pillars in the drama's structure and continuity. Though the poems vary in content, they are united by the theme of Troy's destruction, combined with the Trojan women's sense of loss and desolation.

This song describes the arrival of the wooden horse at the gates of Troy, the people's jubilation because they thought this meant the end of the war, and the terror which followed when the horse discharged the armed Greeks to slaughter the women's husbands in their beds. It would certainly have been one of the high-spots of the tragedy in ancient times. Among the wealth of poetic detail I would specially emphasize the *musical* imagery. The first two lines start in a metre more associated with athletic victory-songs; but this, in the Chorus' words is a *new* song, sung in tears, a *funeral* song, and the rhythm which then takes over follows a strongly insistent lyric iambic pattern. The contrast between triumph and misery is borne out in the different sounds that are described. On the one hand there are the songs of joy which accompanied the admission of the wooden horse; the instrumental music, dancing and shouting at the subsequent feast; the Chorus' own singing and dancing in honour of Artemis. Then the shout of the Greeks rings out as they start to slaughter the population and the children cling to their mothers' dresses.

Scene 4 (lines 568-797) Andromache

The Chorus leader (once again in anapaests) announces the entrance of Andromache, Hector's widow, with her little son Astyanax, on a cart piled high with Trojan spoils.

The Andromache episode starts with what can be fairly called an operatic duet, in which Andromache and Hecuba (in lyric metres) lament antiphonally for their sufferings, the fall of Troy, the death of Hector and Paris' disastrous love for Helen. The duet begins in what are called 'syncopated' iambics, that is iambic phrases of four or six heavy beats with some of the light syllabus omitted, of the pattern: 'My mástérs, the Greéks, leád me cáptíve!' Euripides then asks his two singers to chant a few lines in dactylic hexameters, the metre of Homer's epic, which naturally recalls the most familiar tale of Troy in the *Iliad*. The duet is a powerful beginning to a powerful scene.

The formality of the exchange continues in a passage of *distichomythia*, during which Hecuba tells Andromache of Cassandra's abduction and Andromache reports the sacrifice of Polyxena, enigmatically referred to by Talthybius in Scene 3. This leads on to the first of two long speeches for Andromache in which she contrasts her fate with her sister-in-law's. Polyxena is now dead and immune to suffering, while she herself worked hard to win a reputation as a loyal wife to Hector, only to lose the husband she loved and then to be carried off into slavery. In rhetorical terms this speech is an argument that Polyxena dead is better off than Andromache living; but the Chorus leader speaks of it at the end (684) as a *lament*. It might also be seen as a kind of hymn to the wifely devotion associated with Andromache in the Greek imagination.

Hecuba follows with a further lament of her own. She uses the image of a ship's crew in a storm to describe her own plight. She advises Andromache to accept her new husband's rule, so that she can rear her son Astyanax to lead a revival of Troy in the future. For a moment there seems to be a glimmer of hope, but it is soon to be dashed.

Reenter Talthybius, reluctantly bearing a message for Andromache. Thirteen lines of *stichomythia* build up suspensefully to the revelation that Odysseus has persuaded the Greeks not to allow the child Astyanax to be reared by his mother but to throw him to his death from the walls of Troy. The herald tries to win Andromache's cooperation by a warning that, if she makes trouble, her son's body will go unburied.

Andromache's second aria is even more moving than her first. She weeps over her son as he clings to her dress. Her maternal tenderness recalls Medea's poignant speech to her children before she kills them. The emotion of love then yields to violent anger against the Greeks and against Helen whose beautiful eyes brought death to the plains of Troy. In a furious run of short syllables she orders her foes to carry Astyanax away, to *throw* him and feast on his flesh. With a similar cry to be *thrown* on board herself, she makes a passionate exit.

The tension rises even higher, rather like a drum-roll crescendo, in the scene's concluding anapaests. Talthybius hands over Astyanax to his guards and makes his own exit in distress. The final words go to

Hecuba, who calls after the child as he is marched off and beats her head and breast in a desperate outburst of wild lamentation.

2nd Choral Song (lines 799-859)

After such a gruelling climax, the audience needs some relief and that is what Euripides offers in the choral ode which follows. The subject matter is still the fall of Troy, but treated in a much more detached way than in the preceding ode. The Chorus sings of an earlier sack by earlier Greeks, Telamon and Heracles, when Laomedon was king. They also tell of two Trojan princes, Ganymede and Tithonus who were loved by gods and swept up to Olympus - but they are indifferent to Troy's fate. "The gods' love is lost to Troy."

The poem contains some images of destruction and suffering, but these are contrasted with others of serenity and beauty. The decorative language is complemented by the flowing "dactylo-epitrite" metre associated with the victory odes of the Theban poet Pindar. I suspect that Euripides could well have contrived an elegant and ornate dance for this number, to delight the audience's eyes as well as their ears. At all events, the music clearly trips along with none of the relentless insistence of the iambs in the first choral song.

This song also provides a transition to the totally different mood and atmosphere of the next scene.

Scene 5 (lines 860-1059) Helen

This episode is in a totally different key from the rest of the play. Music gives way to words and to arguments as such. Singing language is forgotten. For those who know Greek, the noun *logos* and the cognate verb *lego* appear no fewer than sixteen times between them.

Menelaus enters to fetch his adulterous wife, Helen, whom the Greeks have given him, either to kill or carry home to Greece. He announces his intention to take her home and kill her there in retribution for the Greeks who fell at Troy. Hecuba approves this, but warns Menelaus against the powers of Helen's beauty; and, sure enough, the *femme fatale* appears, dragged on by guards but elegantly dressed to exert her charms.

Then follows the kind of scene which the Athenian audience found highly entertaining - an *agon* or formal debate between Helen and Hecuba. First Helen advances detailed arguments to justify her elopement with Paris and to prove that the Trojan war has positively benefited Greece. Then Hecuba, in a reply of even greater length, demolishes Helen's arguments and concludes with an appeal to Menelaus to kill his wife as a warning to other faithless women. Menelaus is minded to find Helen guilty and have her stoned at once, but he yields to her pleas to the extent of ordering his attendants to take her down to the ships. She will sail back to Greece - on a different ship from himself.

This scene is an excellent example of Euripides' celebrated "discontinuity of tone". We are no longer in a world of high tragedy but of rhetoric for rhetoric's sake. We can enjoy the ingenious casuistry of the arguments used in the debate and almost forget the horrors of war for a while. Apart from the formal speeches of the three soloists, the dialogue between them is structured in speeches of unequal length, more loosely than in other scenes. Euripides even allows himself a laugh-line. When Hecuba implores Menelaus not to allow Helen to board his own ship (she fears that Helen will save her life by seducing her husband), Menelaus is made to ask, whether seriously or as a joke, "Why? Has she put on weight?"

3rd Choral Song (lines 1060-1122)

This song restores the drama to its dominant mood, as the Chorus accuses Zeus of betraying Troy and ignoring the worship he has received. Once again the women are personally involved in the images of their unburied husbands, their own impending captivity and their children crying out to them as they are abducted. They end by cursing Menelaus and Helen and praying for their destruction by lightning on the sea.

Musically this is a very exciting piece. The first pair of stanzas is composed in regular phrases of four or six strong pulses like the insistent beats of a drum. In the second pair the phrasing is more elaborate, with a splendid succession of four 5/8 bars at a climax in the middle (1091, 1110), shortly followed by a run of five phrases of three heavy beats, building up to a second climax at the end.

Scene 6 (lines 1118-1332)

There follows the magnificent closing scene in which the audience witnesses the solemn rituals paid to Astyanax's dead body, the Greeks setting fire to Troy and its buildings collapsing in ruins. At the very end, the Trojan women depart for their ships to their new life of slavery. If we look at the structure, we may well see this conclusion as music drama of peculiar grandeur.

In a few transitional anapaestic lines, the Chorus leader signals the return of Talthybius with his men, bearing the body of Astyanax on the shield of his father, Hector. In a longish speech of quiet, sympathetic dignity, the herald explains that Andromache has had to leave for Greece quickly with her new husband. Hecuba is entrusted with the task of dressing the child's body for burial, which Talthybius undertakes to perform himself. He leaves to dig the grave.

The ritual mood thus set, Hecuba begins her last great aria. She orders the attendants to lay the shield down and embarks on a long lament for her grandson. Her speech reminds me strongly of Brünnhilde's noble lament for Siegfried at the end of Wagner's *Ring* cycle, before she mounts and sets fire to the hero's pyre. Hecuba's lament has a similar solemnity and pathos; and, as in *The Twilight of the Gods*, it is the prelude to an ultimate catastrophe.

Next, though, we have the dressing of the child's body. The action is accompanied by shortish iambic speeches from Hecuba, punctuated by lyric cries of mourning from the Chorus. (Ancient Greek has some wonderfully effective grief-sounds, such as *e e*, *aiai* and *oimoi*, for which there are no equivalents in English.) Astyanax is now ready for burial and his body is carried off on the shield.

Transitional anapaests are heard for the last time as the Chorus leader expresses sorrow for the dead child and cues in the arrival of officers bearing torches. These Talthybius commands to set fire to the city, so that the Greeks can depart from home; the women are to make their way to the ships when they hear a trumpet sound; Hecuba must follow Odysseus' guards who have come to fetch her. As the old queen prepares to leave, she greets Troy, now imagined in the poetry as already on fire. Suddenly she tries to end her life by running into the flames herself, but she is constrained by the guards.

In the last formal lyric lament between Hecuba and the Chorus (starting with the cry *óttototótotoí*) we may well be reminded again of Wagner. The *Ring* ends orchestrally with the Hall of the Gibichungs collapsing, as the flames rise from Siegfried's pyre in a conflagration which finally envelops the Nordic gods themselves in their castle on Valhalla. Perhaps the imagination of Wagner, who greatly admired Greek tragedy, was inspired by Euripides' vision at the end of *Trojan Women*. The Greek poet hadn't the resources of a vast orchestra and modern scenery, but the voices and physical movements of his actor and Chorus could have produced an effect in its own terms as overwhelming.

In the first pair of symmetrical stanzas, Hecuba and the Chorus call Zeus to witness the collapse of Troy in fire and smoke. In the second, they kneel on the earth and beat the ground with their hands as they cry to their dead loved ones to take note of their plight. The concluding invocation of Troy and its burning temples reaches its climax in a great crash, like an earthquake, of its falling towers. We cannot know if this was merely suggested by the poetry or accompanied by noises off.

But one sound effect there must surely have been - the long, loud blast of a trumpet, the signal mentioned by Talthybius. The powerful antiphonal wailing is suddenly broken off, and Hecuba faintly orders her trembling limbs to carry her into slavery. "Alas, unhappy city!" is the Chorus' dejected response, as they slowly follow the old queen to the ships and the acting space is left empty.

I have tried in this conspectus of *Trojan Women* to suggest that, in composing it, Euripides exploited the musical and quasi-musical character and conventions of Greek tragedy to a peculiarly marked degree. Apart from the prologue and the Helen scene, his appeal (as in opera or music drama) was more to his audience's emotions than to its intellect. My account depends, of course, on the sound and metrical forms of the ancient text which constitutes the original "score". The effect in modern spoken English is bound to be somewhat different. I hope, though, that my description of Euripides' musical sequence may help newcomers to Greek tragedy to appreciate a little of the emotional experience which this drama would have offered its first audience. *Trojan Women* has other kinds of resonance when viewed in its historical and social setting. Its formal, musical aspect, however, adds a complementary dimension to our engagement with this compelling play from the past, which still has the power, more than 2,400 years later, to move and excite us in the theatre.

Euripides' *Trojan Women*

Extract (slightly adapted) from Chapter 7 of *The Cambridge Companion to Greek Tragedy*, ed. P.E.Easterling, Cambridge 1997 (173-7)

This play deals with the worst that can happen to a city; it has aptly been called "Euripides' *Endgame*". It uses the events of the Trojan War, particularly the last hours before the ultimate firing of the ruins, when the men are already dead, the women waiting to be allocated to their new masters, and the victors preparing to sail home. The play was put on in 415 BC, when the possibility that a Greek city might be annihilated was not at all a remote one for the audience. Plataea, an allied city, hardly more than forty miles from Athens, had been utterly destroyed the year after it capitulated to the Peloponnesians in 427, and at Scione in Chalcidice in 421 and at Melos in 416 the Athenians themselves had put to death all the males of military age and enslaved the rest of the community. Euripides' play, the third in a group on related Trojan themes, must surely have been perceived as suggesting meanings relevant to its own times, but the story of the fall of Troy had special advantages as a myth for all times. Troy was both the most "real" of all ancient cities because of its vivid presence in the *Iliad* and, being non-Greek, the least obviously representative of a contemporary

Greek polis. Even if there had been no risk of its being considered too painful or inflammatory, a play on the fall of a *Greek* city might have seemed intolerably ill-omened, whereas the whole point about Troy was that it fell. But the distance in time and space, and the cast of appropriate heroic characters, in no way reduce the power of the text to challenge and disturb. It is worth looking at some ways in which the play prompts the audience's reactions.

The prologue at once suggests a strong sense of the desolation of the ruined city: Poseidon, the god who was its protector, is on the point of abandoning it: "I am leaving famous Ilion and my altars, for when evil desolation takes hold of a city the things of the gods are sick and not given honour" (25-7). When gods appear on stage in Greek tragedy they always have a quasi-"directorial" role, establishing contact with the audience on a different level from that on which the human characters function, and thus offering ironic perspectives, often on the shape of the action to come, as in *Hippolytus* when Aphrodite, announcing to the audience the arrival of the doomed hero, says, "He does not know that the gates of Hades have been opened for him, and that he looks on the daylight for the last time today" (56-7). Here the directorial role is divided between a pair of deities.

Poseidon first explains what has happened to Troy and the Trojan royal family, and introduces the stage picture: the figure of

Hecuba, already in view of the audience, lying prostrate, overwhelmed by the extremity of her grief. "And this unhappy woman, Hecuba, if anyone wishes to see her, here she is [lit. it is easy] lying in front of the gates, weeping many tears for many causes" (36-8). Then Athena extends the time reference to the future by asking Poseidon to help her take vengeance on the victorious Greeks. She was their champion in the past, but now they have insulted her by failing to punish the violence done to Cassandra by Ajax, son of Oileus. Zeus has promised to send a storm and lend her his thunderbolt; Poseidon is to help by stirring the sea and causing shipwrecks, "so that the Greeks may know in future to respect my shrines and to honour the other gods" (8 5-6). Poseidon agrees at once; for the audience there ought to be no doubt that he means what he says. In the epic story (the Cyclic *Nostoi*, *Returns*) the Greek ships did get wrecked on their way back from Troy; a quite brief sketch of the horrors to come is enough to give the scene intertextual resonance. Thus the prologue creates an ironic framework within which the last hours of Troy are to be viewed.

Poseidon's parting words open out, as lines at ends of scenes often do, beyond the immediate situation: "The man who destroys cities is a fool, and through making desolate temples and tombs, the sacred places of the dead, he himself later meets his ruin" (94-6). These lines give a clear signal that the coming action should be "read" as a cautionary tale, an example for all times and places. But the message is not a simple one: the idea "the winners are also to be losers" is given more weight than any detached assessment of the rights and wrongs of what the two sides have done, and at the end of the play no divine figure offers further explanation. This strongly suggests that no divine explanation exists for the suffering that constitutes the action of the rest of the play.

The role of Hecuba, the archetypal sufferer, is a magnificent one in theatrical terms. From the prologue, where her prostrate figure is pointed out by Poseidon, to the last moment of the play, she is visible to the audience; after the gods' departure she is at the centre of the action, whether as prime singer or speaker or as the character most closely affected by all the other events — by what is happening to Cassandra, Andromache, Astyanax, the city itself. She speaks, chants or sings almost a quarter of the lines of the play; as well as solo song and recitative she takes part in lyric exchanges with the Chorus and Andromache, sings in response to Talthybius' spoken lines, dominates the dialogue scenes and makes four big "set-piece" speeches. She is also at the centre of the stage action: she begins her first chant as she lies on the ground and tries to raise herself (98–121); her first long speech is made from the ground after her collapse at 462; at the end of the play when she is being led off into captivity she tries to throw herself into the fire of the burning city (1282-3). But most often she is seen taking part in ritual: initiating lamentation (143-52), decorating the corpse of Astyanax (1209-34), beating the ground to make contact with the dead Trojans as she leaves the city (1305-7).

The dramatic figure of Hecuba is thus one of power although she typifies weakness; this sense of authority is confirmed in her long speeches, each of which contributes something new to the audience's understanding. The first (466-510) is the most direct. Its theme is her change of fortune from regal state to bereavement and degradation; but it is not only her experience, or the Trojan experience: "Call no successful person fortunate before he dies" (509-510). The second speech (686-708) is shorter and less climactic, placed between Andromache's two much longer ones. It is a brief attempt at consolation, ending with hopes for Troy's recovery through Astyanax, and it is immediately followed by the news that the child is to be thrown from the walls of the city. The whole scene charts the destruction of hope, but Hecuba's speech marks the need felt by sufferers to try to give strength to others. The third and longest of her speeches (969 -1032) is her triumphant reply to Helen's self-defence. The second speaker in an *agôn* normally had the favoured position; Hecuba seems to succeed in persuading Menelaus that Helen deserves a public stoning, but perhaps the triumph is hollow, as the references to future punishment with which the scene ends are contradicted by the familiar episode in the *Odyssey* of Menelaus and Helen happily settled back at home (4.1-305). As in the prologue, there is an invitation to the audience to fill the gaps left by the text; even a spectator ignorant of the *Odyssey* could not feel certain that Menelaus would be able to resist his desire for Helen. The last speech (1156-206) shows Hecuba at her most authoritative as she pronounces a funeral oration over her grandson, concluding with lines that closely echo Poseidon's in the prologue, but this time the "fool" is not the sacker of cities, but the person who feels complacent and secure in good fortune. Once more the equation between winners and losers is what comes out most strongly.

The most intense of all Hecuba's moments of understanding comes at the end of her obsequies for Astyanax: she suddenly stops her antiphonal singing with the Chorus, and prompted by their surprised questions she reflects on the meaning of her sorrows, the sorrows of Troy, "of all cities the most hated by the gods", and the futility of the Trojans' piety, and concludes that without these disasters they would have perished without trace, without "giving subjects of song to the poetry of future generations" (1240-5). These words raise questions about the function of poetry, and indeed of the play itself, all the more so as they are closely modelled on lines spoken by Helen in the *Iliad* (6.357-8). As used by Helen the idea is a bitter one; she and Paris will be sung about to their shame; Hecuba's tone is less unambiguous, but there is no hint of easy consolation in her words, as she goes on to doubt whether the ritual she has just performed has any meaning for the dead (1246-50).

The importance of the Chorus in this play is marked by Poseidon in the prologue: he explains that some of the Trojan women have already been allocated to Greek masters, but those who have not are "in this building here, chosen for the leaders of the army" (32-5). So they are a significant group, although unlike the royal family they have no names, and it is never made clear what will happen to each of them individually. Their role is to provide a context for Hecuba's grief and to share in ritual with her; above all it is they who bring Troy into the play. The difference between actors and chorus is brought out very clearly right at the beginning of the play. Much is made in the first lyric exchange between Hecuba and the women about their anxieties for their own future: they are terrified at the sound of the queen's laments, fearing deportation or death, waiting for news from the herald, dreading being parted from their children, speculating about the Greek cities they may go to (153-229). But when Talthybius arrives with the news that each is to go to a separate master and tells Hecuba to ask for details one by one, the list is exhausted with the royal family: Cassandra, Polyxena, Andromache, Hecuba herself. At 292-93 the Chorus ask "What about me?", but the herald has no reply; all that concerns him now is to have Cassandra fetched out, as Agamemnon's prize, so that he can then take the rest to their masters. No more is heard about the women's destinations until their song at 1089-99, and even then they know nothing further, but this is no marginal group of bystanders, and their presence is a constant reminder of the communal disaster. When they sing about the Wooden Horse and the Greeks coming out of ambush (511—76), or about the sound of the lamentations at Troy (826-32), or about the neglect of worship at the old sacred sites (1059-80), they create for the audience a more tangible sense of the city that has been destroyed than anything in any of the characters' speeches.

The song about the Wooden Horse begins, most unusually for a choral ode in tragedy, with an appeal to the Muse to sing them a new kind of song, a "dirge accompanied by tears". The newness, presumably, is not in the idea of lamentation itself, but in the idea of a dirge for a city. The phrasing also draws attention to the text's own "newness", another reminder of the play as performance, just as the extraordinary parody of a marriage song performed by the "maenad" Cassandra turns into an invitation to Hecuba and the women to join the dance (308-40). For the Chorus and Hecuba, her performance generates only horror; Hecuba tells the women to "answer her wedding songs with tears" (350-1).

Finding the right kind of song to suit the terrible events at Troy is evidently a major issue. A similar question of perspectives is raised by the mad Cassandra, whose interpretation both of events in the Trojan War and of the future is closer to the vantage point of the prologue than anyone else's; but neither Hecuba nor the Chorus nor Talthybius can take the measure of what she says. The old proverbial sayings about the mutability of fortune take on new grimness when they are seen in the context of the destruction of a whole community and its culture, but Hecuba's words at 1240-5 have to be taken into account at the very end of the play, when she leads the women in a farewell ritual for the Trojan dead, beating the ground and calling out to children and husbands. The emphasis is all on loss and annihilation, but at least one statement can be understood differently by an audience brought up on epic poetry. When the Chorus sing that the "name of the land will vanish" and "Troy no longer exists" (1322-24) they are singing for an audience for whom Troy's name has survived.

aod publications

Further collections of essays on the following plays are also available:

Aeschylus	*Agamemnon*
	Choephoroi
Sophocles	*Ajax*
	Antigone
	Oedipus the King
Euripides	*Bacchae*
	Electra
	Hippolytus
	Medea
	Trojan Women

For information about any of these, as well as translations, audiobooks and videos, please contact

actors of dionysus,
26 charlton street, york, uk yo23 1jn

t +44 1904 642 912 • f +44 1904 541 749
e info@actorsofdionysus.com
www.actorsofdionysus.com